Sex, Drugs and Rock Chick

KATE MOSS

First published in
Great Britain in 2008
by Artnik Books
Revised edition, 2009

Artnik Books is an imprint of A Jot Publishing
UK address:
Suite 774, 28 Old Brompton Rd
London SW7 3SS, UK

ISBN   978–1–905382–34–7

Picture research Vassilissa Conway
Edited Nicholas Artsrunik
Pictures REX FEATURES
Design: Jay Huggins

KATE MOSS

Sex, Drugs and a Rock Chick

Brandon Hurst
& Beverley Mason

artnik books

Contents

Introduction   9

1. Kate gets Papped   13

2. A Greengrocer's daughter...
   from Croydon   26

3. Fame beckons with its seductive
   finger   51

4. Down in the Depps   79

6. Putrid Pete   157

7. Hitched to Hince?   183

I can only say
over and over again
"that's
what I
do, I'm
just a *mode*

OTHER BOOKS PUBLISHED BY BRANDON HURST:

The Methuselah Trait, Moose Hill Books, 2006

Keira Knightley, Artnik, 2006

Jimmy Choo, Beyond Black, 2006

Angelina Jolie, A Jot, 2007

'Cocaine is God's way
of telling you you're
making too much money.'
Robin Williams

Who needs blood
when you've got
lipstick - Pete
Doherty's caption
to Kate Moss'
lipstick doodle of
herself.

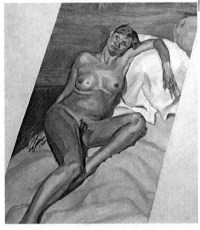

In 2007, the Sunday Times
Rich List estimated Kate
Moss' wealth at £45 million.
Her 2005 'Cocaine Kate' bust
is reckoned to have added
another £10 million to her
fortune.

INTRODUCTION

A Dutch fashion snapper named Inez van Lamsweerde said of Kate Moss:

> 'She's definitely a generation's muse. I can't think of anyone else from our generation whom you'd aspire to look like.'

A generation's muse! Kate Moss has been in the business since she was hand-picked by Storm modelling agency at the age of only fourteen. Her impossibly slim body and languid pout ushered in the new look and attitude embodied by the early '90s, replacing the curvier, more refined models of yesteryear: the Linda Evangelista and Cindy Crawford-type 'Glamazons' of the '80s.

Thanks to her appeal as the Waif and her role in the controversial 'Heroin Chic' movement, she rose meteorically and sensationally through the ranks to the status of Supermodel, featuring in some of the most prominent advertising campaigns of all time. It has made her filthy rich, which has spawned an equally lurid private life.

Yet, according to Kate, her slag-glam look rests on one simple trick of how she looks at the camera. In 2001, she confided to Pearl Lowe, 'You know all I do is look at the lens like it was a big cock I wanna suck. That's what I do.'

This trick has turned Kate Moss into the most professionally photographed woman on the planet. Over a period of 20 years, she has appeared on more than 300 magazine covers, earning many millions of pounds in the process. Yet for all this, if there is one picture that Kate Moss will always be remembered for, it is the one taken by a low-life pal of one of Pete Doherty's nest of vipers, published on the front page of the Daily Mirror on September 15th, 2005.

The image was a grainy still from a video taken on a cam mobile, rather than a scene carefully posed and lit by the professional photographers that she is used to, but both the woman in the shot and what she was doing were unmistakeable. Her legs, bare from the bottom of a tiny miniskirt to her knee-height boots, looked as stunning as ever. But, on this occasion, it was her hands that really drew the eye as she focused on the delicate task of chopping and divying up into lines a pile of lumpy white powder.

The story that broke was part of a press vendetta, the culmination of a long-term desire to expose the world's most famous supermodel and finally prove to the public what the media had long known, but never been able to stand up. The headline was 'Cocaine Kate' and, although the pictures were shot by an amateur using a camera mobile, Kate had been well and truly papped.

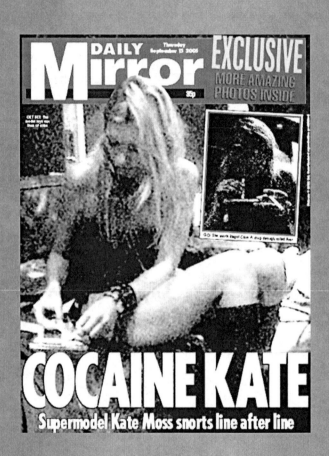

1. KATE GETS PAPPED

The setting is Metropolis Studios in Chiswick, where Pete
Doherty's band Babyshambles were supposed to be finishing
their album. Producer Mick Jones had given up hope of
getting much done again that day. He'd grown used to
indulging Doherty, having done two albums with him already.
In the process he earned the title of honorary Libertine,
as much for his boozing and tolerance of the ubiquitous
drug abuse as for his promotion of our pied piper of the
post-modern generation.

If Mick has any issue with a 31-year-old rock-chick hanging round the studio, he's not going to mention it. She's not exactly encouraging the band to record or at least experiment with guitar riffs, but with an album this many months over the deadline it's just a step in a marathon catch-up. Mick might make the odd chippy comment – just to let the guys know he's not overawed – but, in general, you keep the talent happy. Especially as the lead talent is Peter Pan Doherty with Kate as his Arcadian shepherdess, the girl who inspires the poetic idylls and entrancing melodies. Mick can feel the panicked record company breathing down his neck and the last thing he needs is a stroppy Doherty storming out and going on another ten-day smack bender because his Super-Groupie got blackballed.

Babyshambles playing a 2005 gig

Mick swigs Stella from the can, plays with the slides on the mixer and waits for Kate to get round to chopping up the charlie. At least he might get a line out of her; it's been another long night of sitting around going nowhere. Meanwhile, the rest of the band are getting on with their own thing. Not the recording, obviously - just the endless business of staring, smoking, forming huddles with hangers-on, picking up cans to see which ones still have beer in the bottom, and generally making it look like they're not thinking about when they're going to get a line. The studio is all jittery, like everyone's waiting for the dealer to arrive. This time it's Kate: she's always holding.

People have been in and out all day. Guitarists going AWOL, friends dropping by, friends outstaying their welcome, obscure punk ringtones tripping from mobiles. Some of the guests have been there on business, so to speak, but it's clear by this stage that unless the lady does it herself the only one with the rank to move to the next scene is Pete. Significant glances are going his way but they don't penetrate his concentration as he sits on a sofa trying to shape a chord sequence on his guitar for one of the tracks.

It's not like Coldplay here, where Chris and Gwyneth lead separate lives from the band in hermetically-sealed, drugless private suites. Here, Kate gets by because she is right on the Babyshambles wavelength - she wouldn't last a second in their company if she wasn't. She knows the rules of studio politics as well as she knows how to glide down

Pete Doherty and Kate Moss at the
Isle of Wight music festival June 2005

the catwalk; after all, she's been doing rock videos for
longer than most of these Camden posers have known how to
hold their instruments. She may be a catwalk model but,
as a rock chick, Kate has pedigree. She has performed a
steamy pole-dance on the White Stripes track 'I don't know
what to do with myself' (which, from the way she caresses
herself, must be the sexiest irony that Jack White is ever
going to lay down on a track). She has been shot in the
head for a Johnny Cash album and even did the vocals for
Primal Scream's cover of 'Some Velvet Morning'.

Besides, it's the end of the day now. The human chaff has
gradually peeled away, leaving just the inner circle, the
ones she can trust. She dips into her Hermés Birkin handbag
and pulls out what they've all been waiting for. It's another
bag, tiny and made of plain cling film wrapped around about
five grammes of the old Bolivian Marching Powder. Kate buys
in bulk since models traditionally have to walk a long way
without eating.

A few of the guys are fiddling with their mobiles, texting
their girlfriends or killing time. Band manager James
Mullord always seems to be out of it anyway, so no one
bats an eyelid. Kate starts chopping and chatting, visibly
animated by the start of her familiar ceremony. She's using
a CD-R copy of the album to rack up: just rough mixes, and
some masters from the earlier sessions, but still gold dust
to anyone actually interested in the music. Mick asks her
if she likes how the album's soundi ng. 'Nah, I haven't

heard it,' she sniffs. The CD would be a bit of a scoop if it fell into the wrong hands, as will the video being surreptitiously shot on the palmed mobile. It's right in her face at times, but she's oblivious.

Too much chat and not enough gak for some of the lads. Patrick and Drew, Babyshambles guitar and bass, are getting impatient. Someone comes across and tries to take control of the stash. 'I'll do it, I'll do it,' snaps back Kate, and she's not kidding. Her pride's been challenged in front of the notorious Class A specialists present, and she quickly and smoothly lines up the powder with the efficiency and professionalism that the Daily Mirror would in due course describe as the expertise of a practised user. Not content to be merely a face that launched a thousand ships, she has the hand that chopped out a thousand lines.

Over the course of the next forty minutes Kate would talk rubbish and bang lines like a kid knocking back Smarties. Everyone from producer to opportunist freeloader would jostle for some nose powder. In that time Kate would dole out twenty lines in lightning-quick rounds, including five fat ones for herself. She would duly liven up and come out with the usual banalities about how she didn't smoke grass any more, about the time she tried skunk and pulled a whitey. In fact, she seemed to speak with the openness of someone who trusted her company enough to start boasting. This is one thing charlie is good at - making people talk. The point about this particular drug is that not only does the users think what they're saying is fascinating, but so also do their listeners - as long as they are on gear, too. This is the magic of cocaine.

Kate is renowned for a lot of things. What she is not known for is her scintillating conversation and diamond wit. Even those who swear by her would be hard pressed to testify to it. Yet Kate is one of an extremely rare breed of glitterati: those who know their limitations. The reason she rarely says anything in public is that she knows it would kill the mystique. Kate is all enigma.

Her enigma is a class act: behind her all-knowing look is nothing much at all, except the certainty that for her act to carry any conviction, the first thing she has to do is keep her mouth shut.

One week later and the bidding for the clandestine video was over. The pictures of those forty famous minutes, taken secretly by an insider, had been sold for £150,000 to the Daily Mirror. It was no coincidence that this was the sister paper of the Sunday Mirror, the tabloid which Kate successfully sued for a similar amount in June of the same year. The story? A completely unfounded and libellous allegation relating to the model's supposed cocaine habit. This time, the Mirror Group took no chances. The story wouldn't come out until it had been legalled to high heaven. Nevertheless, when The Mirror insiders saw the pictures they 'beamed with 100 per cent-proof rapture'.

Five days after they had them, the The Mirror splashed. The story went round the world: it was a sensational scoop. The picture on the front page of her chopping out lines was destined to become more iconic than any taken by Mario Testino or Juergen Teller.

Kate's response publicly was to do what she always does: stay stum. Back home there was a witch-hunt to finger the amateur paparazzo among the Babyshamblers and associated hangers-on. Meanwhile, it looked very much like Kate had blotted her copybook with an ink-stain that would indelibly mark her future career. Bizarrely, though, one of the unpredictable consequences of the exposé was that - after the inevitable initial slump in her fortunes - she bounced back bigger than ever.

Fortunately for all the coke-snorters, without admissions from the parties concerned or evidence from the man who shot it, the video of drug taking alone would not be enough to convict in an English court. Nobody was even charged, never mind found guilty. On the other hand, trial by media operates on a much lower standard of proof, and Kate and

Pete's culpability was never in doubt. In any case, she was a beautiful, good-natured blonde girl who had been led astray by a heroin-addled rock'n'roller. Doherty was the fall guy and this, as one friend put it, 'could be the best thing that ever happened to her'. It seemed that she would surely dump him for his treachery - which of course she did, though not immediately and, for about eighteen months, not permanently.

Although it is widely assumed that Kate ditched junkie Pete either to help her get clean (if you believe in fairy-stories) or to save her career (if you're a natural cynic), the truth, while touching on both of these areas, lies in Kate's own pool of neuroses. The Kate Moss story is a study in the loss of control that she succumbed to after breaking up from Johnny Depp in 1998.

It was with Johnny Depp that Kate made her introductions to the rock'n'roll set that has coloured her life since: a time of eternal adolescence with very adult vices. As a bona fide Hollywood star and hell-raiser, the moody Depp was a rarity on the scene: someone who eclipsed Brit-rockers Oasis or Bobby Gillespie in celebrity cool, and who even a supermodel could look up to in terms of sheer glamour - indeed, beauty too. Kate was obsessed and, after a four-year romance, devastated to lose him; she later admitted (in an interview to the man who was to become the father of her child, Dazed and Confused editor Jefferson Hack), that no man since could hope to live up to him.

The immediate aftermath of the Johnny Depp split was heartbreak and rehab, the first public admission of a lifestyle problem. She admitted to too much 'partying', which is a glitterati euphemism for too much charlie. For the public record, it was only for drink (though the Priory, one of her favourite rehab clinics, does deal with problems across the whole spectrum of mood-altering substances).

When Kate emerged, one thing alone was clear: she would never be dumped again, would never again allow the public to see her as the heartbroken victim. She even gave up modelling, at least for a couple of months. Kate also made one of the most memorable comments that she will ever give: 'I quit because I thought, "I hate it". It's mind-numbing, repeating yourself like Groundhog Day.'

Since then Kate Moss has taken an iron grip on her career, her friends and her love-life: no media, no interviews, no projection of her personality beyond the picture-perfect image of the many magazine covers. The part of her that screams out loud for decadence and abandon is unleashed only behind closed doors, channelled into chemicals and sex with anyone she fancies. At her homes in Primrose Hill and in the Cotswolds, Kate rules what Jude Law calls the 'Moss Posse', using her considerable sexual power and social cachet. Here, she allows herself to be adored, letting some people close but leaving most with their noses pressed against the shop window, keeping some women's husbands and sometimes other men's wives at her beck and call.

And, with it all, she turns up on time for every job, always looking beautiful (well, certainly after the army of make-up artists, hair-stylists and Photoshoppers have done their work), scowling sexily for shoots but smiling enigmatically for photographers, charming an entire industry with her professionalism while terrifying her own circle with her quick temper and fickle favour. As a result she has sustained a career at the top of her game for far longer than any of the so-called supermodels, building up her multi-million pound fortune without public scandal until the Daily Mirror bought the papped shots of her and swung a wrecking ball at her, to that moment, seemingly impregnable redoubt.

Once the 'Cocaine Kate' headlines had well and truly settled, she did something else that nobody had predicted. Everyone thought Pete and Kate were ancient history, but she took him back. The question of why has never been answered satisfactorily. It really does seem that she genuinely loved Pete, that she was just as addicted to his personality and talent as he is to his own broad range of vices. Then again, there are those cold-hearted cynics who think the only thing she could want with a druggie and a loser who is never out of the tabloids was a boost to a career that was hurtling towards its sell-by date. Thirty-two wasn't so far off retirement age for the average supermodel. And then, of course, there's the theory that Pete's extensive wild streak reminded her of the lost love of her life, a certain Mr Johnny Depp.

Kate as a 6-year-old in Croydon

2 A GREENGROCER'S DAUGHTER... FROM CROYDON

Kate's tale is a classic one of rags to glad-rags. Her background was nothing special, and there was little to suggest that she might one day become the world's most famous and infamous fashion icon, and now brand. Linda, Kate's mother, was from a solid working-class background. 'My parents were greengrocers,' she said. 'It was a very ordinary life. I was growing up in the sixties, with the Beatles and Carnaby Street, but we never saw any of that. I was just the greengrocer's daughter living south of London. I served fruit and veg on the stall.'

Linda left school at sixteen to work first in a clothes shop, then as an assistant to a knitwear designer. In 1971, when she was nineteen, she married Peter Moss, an airline clerk from Cheam, Sutton. The couple had Kate in 1974. It was all very ordinary until seventeen years later, when her world was abruptly turned upside down by two things. Linda's decision to leave her husband for another man came shortly before her daughter's astonishing rise to fame as one of the world's most famous women.

Kate hails from Croydon, a concrete shopping and industrial centre near London, famous for its alleged provincialism and Chav-like mentality. Croydonians have the flat accent and dull speech patterns of Estuary English which, people say, betrays a deadly suburban small-mindedness. There is even a hairstyle named after the town and its female denizens which is meant to denote an inane mind set: 'The Croydon Facelift' - putting your hair into a pony tail so tight that it pulls the skin back from your face. Croydon girls are legendary for wearing white stiletto heels and going out on the town with ultra-short skirts and no tights, even in the middle of winter.

'In modelling, you need something more than just the ability to look good, but Kate Moss is the exception in that she is only about looking good,' says American Janice Dickinson, arguably the first supermodel. 'She has those two looks: hair up or hair down, with lots of leg showing and she looks phenomenal.' That's Croydon all over: a cultural lowest common denominator. It's hardly surprising that millions of women identify with and aspire to be her in some measure.

Kate's parents say she liked to dress up as a child but was shy in ballet classes. She wasn't a show off, just sort of blended into the background. 'I was quite shy at school,' she said. 'I was the girl the boys wanted to be friends with, not the girl the boys fancied. I didn't really have a boyfriend.' She would make up for lost time later. Some teenagers are different though, just set apart from the rest, no matter what their upbringing. These are destined to break away from the pack and achieve something unique, for better or worse. Kate was one of them, and she had both the ambition and the talent to make good.

There's more to it than just talent, though. Like other young success stories, Kate Moss's history possesses another vital feature: a strong work ethic. Kate might have her problems, but going to work isn't one of them. 'There was always something special about Kate,' said her dad back in 1994. 'If you ask her what she might have done if the modelling hadn't happened, she'll say she would have worked in a shop in Croydon. But if she's really honest with herself, Kate knows that somehow she would have done well.'

BREAKING UP

Kate Moss's childhood wasn't without its troubles. Peter and Linda Moss were an outwardly happy couple who appeared to have it all - each other, material success and two beautiful children. Kate was born in 1974, then they had a son Nick, born two years later. Whilst Peter Moss worked in the travel industry, Linda stayed at home as a housewife. Then something happened which destroyed the dream. Bored with her life and finding her marriage 'too safe and mundane', Linda Moss took a job in a pub. It was there, in 1987, that she met Geoff Collman.

Geoff Collman was a flashy entrepreneur with a natural ability to make money - in a friend's words, 'a white collar

Del Boy Trotter who drove a Porsche instead of a Reliant Robin.' Collman was an exciting bad boy who made Linda Moss feel special. She was in her thirties and feeling like life was passing her by. Geoff Collman was everything Peter Moss wasn't (those who know him say he is a kind-hearted and loyal man - a safe, reliable, run-of-the-mill kind of guy). 'Geoff Collman had the gift of the gab, was good-looking in a roguish sort of way, had tattoos and was a bit of a Jack the Lad,' a friend told the Daily Mail. 'Linda couldn't resist him and she began a passionate affair.'

When his wife asked Peter Moss for a trial separation, he thought that she simply needed some space to sort her head out and would then come back to him, believing she was just temporarily bored and dissatisfied with her life. He was devastated when he discovered his wife's affair with Collman. The fallout was explosive and resulted in the end of the marriage, with Linda Moss going to live with her new lover, along with Kate.

Kate's brother Nick chose to go with their father. It's difficult to ascertain exactly what happened to Geoff Collman. Apparently Linda Moss was with him for a time, but no longer. She now lives alone in a house Kate bought for her. Peter Moss has remarried, with more children, and has his own travel business, which his daughter also helped to finance. Kate's parents still speak but are not close. The separation was a monumental bust up with 'lots of heated arguments and one massive screaming match when it finally came to an end,' says a family friend. 'Modelling offered her an escape. I think seeing her parents' marriage fail had a big effect on her. She finds it hard to commit because she saw this failure at such a young age.'

'So she always chooses destructive relationships.'

Kate's mother, 56, has recently come out as a sort of celebrity herself - especially since the drugs bust. According to the London Evening Standard, a thirty-something American neighbour called Brad has become her 'walker' - media speak

for a platonic companion - and she spends a lot of time with him. She has the same slouchy-hipped walk, high cheekbones and wide-spaced eyes that Kate inherited. An addiction to Marlboro Lights also appears to be a family trait, which might go some way to explaining the non-preachy way she allowed her willful daughter to indulge.

Kate with her mother Linda after The Mirror's Cocaine Kate scoop

Linda Moss is now pursuing 'me time', as it's euphemistically phrased, the stage of life when many older women have realised that both children and romantic relationships have played havoc with your sense of self - especially if you have sacrificed yourself for one or the other and feel your own needs have been put on the back burner. 'When you get older and your children move on, then you have the time to do things you always wanted.' Maybe that's why she felt the need to depart from her solid life as a housewife twenty years ago, when she made her fateful choice.

Linda Moss's young life was a far cry from the 'world is your oyster' lifestyle that her daughter enjoyed as a teenager, perhaps the reason why she was so willing for Kate to pursue a modelling career at such a young age.

At only thirteen years old, Kate was devastated by her parents' separation. That, and being discovered by a modelling agency at JFK airport a year later, propelled her from an average prepubescent into a semi-mythical being without the chance to establish a 'normal' persona in between. It very likely had more than a little to do with her future wild, irresponsible behaviour, not to mention her choice of men. After all, she had no strong male role models. Like her mother, she would follow the pattern of dumping the stable, responsible partner to chase after the unpredictable and destructive bad-boy types. She has a penchant for those Hommes Fatales, the Byronic men dressed in black, epitomised by her relationship with the then wild boy Johnny Depp, back in the nineties. Since Depp, she has proved the 'like mother, like daughter' axiom by deserting the sober, down-to-earth Jefferson Hack, father of her daughter Lila, and chasing after a string of mad, bad and dangerous-to-know types. (Pete Doherty being, she hopes, the last of these).

At the time of her parents' separation, Kate was still attending Riddlesdown High School in Croydon. Friends remember her 'going off the rails at that point', disappearing with unsuitable boys. There is nothing to suggest that Kate wouldn't have turned into a dissolute party girl even if she hadn't been thrust so forcefully into the fickle celebrity market at such a young age. She'd had plenty of practice at it beforehand - she has admitted as much. When she checked into the Priory rehab clinic in 1999 (never specifying exactly what ailed her at the time) she said: 'I can't blame the shape my life has taken all on modelling. I'd probably have got there in the end anyway. Modelling just speeded things along.'

At school she was never interested in studying and rarely bothered with such distractions as homework. 'My favourite subject at school was English and Drama because you never had to do anything,' she openly admits. 'And I never did games. I had a period every week. We'd just have a smoke at the back of the gym.' School was merely a social centre. 'We used to go to people's houses and steal their Mum's booze,' she says, recalling those halcyon days when life was so uncomplicated. 'On the way to school. Anytime. Some bloke would have brought it in a bag from his Dad's stash - we'd smoke and drink Super Tennants. I was smoking pot then too.'

This behaviour would seem less worrying if you didn't know she was in her early teens at the time. 'We used to go into

Tesco and nick things,' she said. 'Well, I never could do it but my friends used to and I'd stand there and watch.' The recent family upheaval meant that parental supervision was sparse. 'Literally, my parents let us do what we wanted,' she said. 'I was smoking when I was thirteen in front of my parents, and drinking. I'd have parties when I'd come in at three o'clock in the morning because someone chucked me out then.' Then she added, 'It's actually worked to my benefit, because you end up thinking for yourself because you know you're not rebelling against anything.'

Most girls have a bit of the wild child in them at that age, but grow out of it before too long. Typically some boy comes along and you go with the flow, maybe get serious with the relationship; you get a job or go abroad for a gap year backpacking; perhaps you might try university or college to learn some useful skill to stand you in good stead. It's hard to imagine Kate Moss doing any of those. She would have been more likely to run away to join the circus - which, in a sense, she did. 'I wanted to travel,' she explained, 'but I didn't know how. I thought I'd go to college and do travel tourism or something boring like that. God, I'm glad I didn't. I'd be in a travel agent's behind a desk by now.'

The Croydon wild-child was always going to grab the chances Kate was to be offered. Being given a free hand at such a young age taught her to be bold. 'It was much more fun to be naugh-teee!' After she started modelling, school became a lost cause. 'I kind of lost interest - not that I was that interested in the first place.' Janice Dickinson, the former American supermodel turned TV presenter, offers her informed take on Kate Moss:

'She's basically a little girl inside and doesn't know any better.'

Dickinson possesses impeccable credentials to comment on Kate's predicament: she was once the mother of all bad girls, notorious for her riotous lifestyle, hard partying and 'revolving door' bedroom policy.

Dickinson was the Eve from which the others sprang: the mother of the 'Glamazon' race of models that preceded the look ushered in by Kate's rise. These 'Supers' - tall, curvy, over-styled divas, later to include the likes of Linda Evangelista, Cindy Crawford and Christie Brinkley - were supposed to be inspirational, but often ended up making women feel just as inadequate as today's 'size zeros' or 'lollipops' do. When they fell, as some of them inevitably did, it made everyone feel so much better that even the chosen few could screw their lives up so spectacularly.

Kate Moss is very much on Dickinson's mind as she explains how beautiful women must be humbled as a punishment for their beauty, fame and success by falling from grace and then gaining redemption through humility and contrition.

However, she's not one to excuse the likes of Kate. First of all the English model has displayed none of the public remorse required of the newly-humbled - apart from a short, generalised statement saying that she 'took responsibility for her actions.' ('I also accept that there are various personal issues that I need to address and have started taking the difficult, yet necessary, steps to resolve them,' was Kate's only mea culpa. Dickinson is a disciple of the Minnesota 12-Step and the first step to recovery is owning up to the fact that you are screwed up.)

'If you were discovered at an early age like Kate Moss then of course you'll end up messed up emotionally,' Janice states.

Asked if Kate is a basket case underneath the cool exterior, she replied, 'Are you kidding me?! Inside she's still only fourteen years old, the age she was discovered. She's never had to grow up.'

MODEL CHILD

It's a dreamy teenage girl's classic fantasy. Some stranger comes up to you in the street and says: 'Hey, have you ever thought about being a model?' (Many a pretty starstruck ingénue has been conned by the implicit flattery as well: 'Pay us a grand and we'll make you into another Cindy/ Linda/ Helena...') It's not surprising that Kate was a little wary when, in 1988, a man came up to her and delivered his pitch. His name was Simon Chambers and he was the brother of Sarah Doukas, a former model and all-round entrepreneur who had recently started her own modelling agency, Storm, in London. Storm was unashamedly elitist and had the reputation of taking only the very best models. 'We used to turn people down who were actually quite good because I wanted to create a very elitist agency and work only with the high-end magazines. I always think you have to strive for the top,' she told the Sunday Times. Storm was also well-known for finding models in odd places.

At fourteen, Kate didn't think she had what it took to be a model (neither did her sceptical mother) but then, compared to the Glamazons, no one did. 'I was quite thin but not tall for a model,' said Kate about her anti-Supermodel teenage image. 'I was kind of lanky. People would say "Oh, you should be a model" or something like that. But I'd never really considered it. In fact I thought it was quite vain to say that I want to be a model.'

But the modelling industry was about to hit a reality check. In the '80s, the fashionable female image was either the blokey, power-dressing career women with big shoulders, or else the artificial glamour and gross excess of the Supers. The '90s zeitgeist was beginning to take into consideration the harsh political and economic truth of the times. Bought with the stacks of money that were being made on the global currency markets, excessive flamboyance was now seen as distasteful.

After the stock market crash of the late '80s, people started to turn away from the 'greed is good' culture. What they wanted was to be accepted for themselves, something that was anti-glamour, anti-money: something authentic. They wanted a new reality, though the one they got was still centred on women's bodies and just as physically and psychologically damaging as the old one.

Sarah Doukas had originally been a booker for IMG but had struck out on her own to start a new agency. She secured funding from Richard Branson, whose wife Lindy she had once shared a flat with. Innovative model agents like Doukas took the view that you couldn't expect the next big thing to just walk into your office - you had to go out into the world and find it. Scouting for girls on the street was the new way to capture the spirit of the age, a step back from the hard-edged artifice that had dominated the fashion industry for so long. Doukas and her brother had been talent-searching in America but had drawn a big, fat zilch.

Kate Moss with Sarah Doukas at a 1998 Storm Model Agency thrash in London

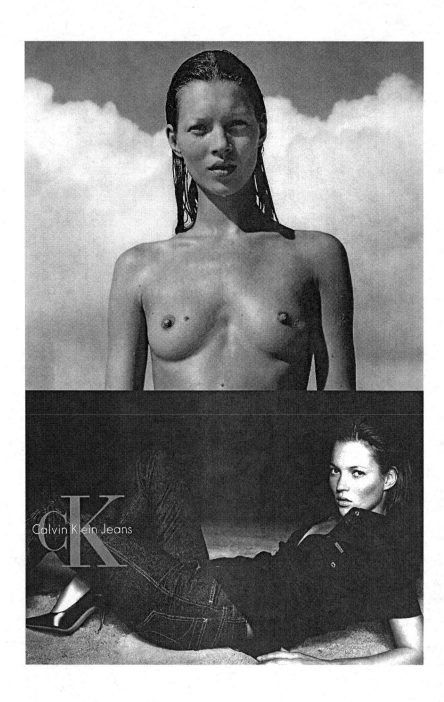

Resigned to the fact that the trip had been a waste of time, they were therefore understandably excited when they saw Kate for the first time. Her unusual face - all high cheek bones, broad, flat nose, spiky teeth and wide-spaced eyes - and her famous skinny body with its bandy legs and no breasts, would come to incarnate the controversial but still inchoate raw, edgy, anti-fashion philosophy that was going to burst out and hit the front pages with such spectacular success a few years later. It was an image as far removed from the Supers as it was possible to get. Kate was to define what culture was to become: undisciplined individuality as art.

Because of her background - wild girl on the run from discipline and conformity - the burgeoning icon was streetwise but naive at the same time, an ideal combination of sexuality and innocence. This was the quality which would come to define a generation: you have the smarts, you're still open to the possibilities of the new world you're about to inhabit, yet you couldn't care less about it. It wasn't like the '60s - no one thought about changing the world any more. There was a streak of nihilism and individualism a mile wide.

Doukas and her brother, Simon Chambers, spotted their protégé in the Virgin Atlantic standby queue, pleading for mercy in order to get back to England. The fourteen-year-old Kate had been on a two-week holiday with her father and brother in the Bahamas, but the family had ended up

stranded at JFK airport for three days, unable to get a seat
on a plane. There was a family wedding to attend - Peter
Moss's sister was getting married the next day - and Kate
was using this to argue the family case at the check-in. The
sob story must have worked because the family were informed
that there was one last flight with three seats left: one in
first class, one in business and one in economy. Kate took
the economy seat. As fate would have it, it was the same
plane that Sarah Doukas and her brother were boarding. On
the flight, Chambers approached her. 'Excuse me, but have
you ever thought about being a model?' he asked. Twenty-one
years later, Kate is still with Storm.

The holiday was memorable for another reason, as Kate later
confessed. 'I lost my virginity on that holiday in the
Bahamas. Rather that than having it taken by some boy in
Croydon.' Kate's awakening sexuality coincided with her new
image: she was about to epitomise the fashion world's new
version of Lolita - the starving orphan, a grubby nymphet
in a pair of cheap nylon knickers from Woolies, who looks
as if she should be at home playing with her dolls, instead
of smoking a joint and swigging a can of Stella.

Kate's parents were understandably wary about this bolt
from the blue. Sex slave trafficking, financial rip-offs
and all sorts of other fates-worse-than-death must spring
to mind when some strange man comes up to your teenage
daughter and offers to make her a star. When Kate told her
father about the encounter as they got off the plane, he

was predictably cagey. 'I was taken aback,' Peter said. 'I'd never thought of my daughter as extraordinary.'

Perhaps he was just naive; as a middle-aged man accompanied by a young girl, people had already jumped to other conclusions. 'Thinking back on that holiday, someone did comment that they thought I was a dirty old man for having such a pretty, young wife!' Back in Croydon, the family debated the offer. Linda Moss was unimpressed; after all, teenage girls are otherwise warned off these sorts of lines. 'She thought it was a major con,' said Kate. 'She was saying, "Oh, yeah, they'll want like ten grand, then they'll take a few pictures and that'll be it."'

In the end, Linda did take her daughter up to the Storm offices in London. They took a few Polaroids (at no cost to Kate or Linda), put them in a book and signed her up. Afterwards, Linda said, 'If you want to do this, you're on your own because I'm not traipsing around London ever again like that. It's a nightmare.' Kate didn't feel the same way. 'I was really excited, it didn't feel beyond my reach, really.' It must have felt like Christmas was coming round every day.

She got into it straight away, not least because she was still at school and the frequent trips to London for castings and go-sees gave her the freedom to play truant - not to mention the job's perks. 'I'd go on the train to castings,' she said. 'Changing from my school uniform on the train. I

carried on like that for a few years, getting jobs in bits and pieces.' It was like a dream. At the age of fourteen she had a licence to go charging round London, mingling with other people who would soon cause a revolution in fashion, pop, style, and art. She was there at the beginning of a whole new world-view which was turning everything on its head. It all started with editorial photography, so quirky

A 19-year-old Kate Moss in 1993 sitting in the Café de Flore on Boulevard Saint-Germain where John-Paul Sartre wrote one of the great rallying cries for liberté: 'Man is condemned to be free.'

faces and bodies were paramount. Having said that, Kate's first modelling assignment was for a facial scrub advert in Mizz magazine. She was paid £150 – peanuts by the industry's standards – but still not bad for a 14-year-old. She didn't blow it on a dress either: Kate had learnt a kind of shop-keeper mentality from her mother and was always careful with money. She can be generous but never profligate.

It would get a lot more lucrative very quickly as Kate immersed herself in the business of modelling and the world that came with it. Her baptism-by-fire to both the catwalk and the fashion world's excesses came in her first show at the age of fifteen, when she was cast as Lolita by John Galliano.

The trip involved some hard partying and a lot of serious drinking - not that she remembered much of it by the end.

Kate decided to take some time off school for the show, staying with one of the seamstresses. 'I had to come down the catwalk by myself. It looked huge, like an air plane runway. I was so nervous,' she remembers. After the show, everyone involved went back to Galliano's apartment to watch the video. 'Someone had run off with the champagne so me and this other person drank a bottle of Scotch between

Shoot on London's Millennium Bridge in June 2002

us. I passed out at the table and went missing for two days. I was supposed to be back at school but no-one knew where I was.' (In a hotel throwing up, as it happens.)

In an industry that conveniently turns a blind eye to what it disingenuously refers to as 'high spirits', this introduction to the delights of alcohol poisoning was an entirely normal occurrence. 'For years I never thought there was anything wrong with it,' she said. 'We all used to get drunk at the shows. I just thought I was having a really good time, which I was. But it got too much. There was no normality. I felt like everyone was sucking me away.' You can imagine the manic energy required for all the shows, and with mentors like Naomi Campbell and Donatella Versace (who recently went into rehab for cocaine addiction herself), it's a wonder that she managed to survive it all. Of these early catwalk shows, she said:

'I loved it. When I met Naomi and Christy [Turlington], they took me under their wing; we had so much fun. The Galliano shows! It was amazing, like a high – the adrenaline, and "You're on,

and you're going to be this and do that!"'

She explained how Galliano ran the show: 'John tells you your character, and you just get so into it because of the energy.' Not to mention the after-show scene. 'It was Versace, and parties every night; every night there was something you had to go to - and then you had to be up at six. I mean it was fun!'

Some say the catwalk-show scene has changed since then. When Kate dipped her toes back into the water recently she was disappointed to find that things were different. 'I was like, "What's going on tonight then?" and they're all going to bed! This is what my booker tells me in Paris: Nobody goes out.' There are still high-energy scenes like the ones Kate enjoyed so much, but with more models having children and designers themselves tending towards the more stable, down to earth types like Stella McCartney and Phoebe Philo, Kate may be one of the last of her kind from the crazy hey-day of '80s and '90s fashion excess. Many still do fall by the wayside, of course, but for different reasons; the business is so competitive and the turnover so high that the girls have to look after themselves to keep up.

'A new economics rules the scene now,' Kate said in a Vogue interview. 'These days I think it's because there are so many new girls coming so quickly; they don't last more than a season, so I suppose they think, "To stay where I am, I'm going to have to take care of myself, be on time at work and get sleep." When I was eighteen, I was "La-la la - two hours, fine!" It didn't affect me really then.'

There was more to it than that, though. It wasn't just that she was able to sustain that kind of pace and schedule. Kate seemed to want and need the excitement and perpetual high, in work and her private life. If she couldn't find it in one, she'd get it in the other.

Kate has never come clean about her real party lifestyle. She makes no secret of the fact that she drank and smoked heavily - it's hardly illegal, after all - but never admitted to taking Class A drugs like cocaine and heroin. There were always hints and whispers about her excessive fondness for the harder stuff, but nobody could prove it and she could be extremely litigious if they tried. (She successfully sued the Sunday Mirror in 2005 for saying she had collapsed in a drug-induced coma. Its daily sister paper, in turn, were understandably rather pleased when it had the opportunity to publish photos of her hoovering up the charlie later that same year.)

At this stage, however, her habits weren't a problem. She was moving up in the world, her drug usage was contained and her life had not yet been subjected to the kind of media focus that puts your life under the paparazzi's flash and magnifying lens.

As an up-and-coming teen
sensation, she was happy
to live life to the full
and not worry about the
consequences... until they
arrived.

3. Fame beckons with its seductive finger

Wallis Simpson, the woman for whom Edward VIII gave up the throne, once said, 'You can never be too rich or too thin'. She certainly knew a bit about both, but Kate's critics would doubtless argue with that statement; at 7½ stone, at 5 foot 7 and a size 8, Kate has come under heavy fire for promoting an image that many have copied to the detriment of their health. Before the '90s, supermodels had never been so thin, and it is hard to overestimate the impact Kate made on the world when she began to appear in the phenomenally successful Calvin Klein Obsession ads in 1993. Unless you witnessed them, there is just no way to explain the appeal of her controversial look. Her slim, almost anorexic-looking body became legendary. She was 'Minnie' Moss, the 'Superwaif', a byword for fragility and an instantly recognisable cultural reference.

She had her detractors, of course. Plus-sized comedienne Dawn French quipped, 'Reubens would have painted me, using Kate Moss as a paintbrush.' Others utterly failed to see any funny side, and levelled their criticism at the fashion industry that was making money out of her supposed emaciation and 'underage' baby-doll sexual allure. A fashion magazine editorial called Baby Belle wrote, 'The strongest trend from the catwalks is the girly look. Think short, think frocks, think schoolgirl charm.'

Schoolgirl charm is fine if you're fifteen, but one of the pictures showed Kate as jailbait, propped up against a bar sipping a glass of wine. The concept of the infantilisation of women is nothing new, but the industry's in-your-face presentation of what was ostensibly illegally young sexuality crossed the lines of decency for too many people. The 'Heroin Chic' look, which glamorised the thin, strung-out appearance, went hand-in-hand with it, and did her almost as few favours.

Today, Kate's impossibly thin figure has been vindicated by many years of intense popularity. Although the simple fact of growing up meant that she has left behind the Lolita look of her early years - after it propelled her to fame in simultaneous slews of admiration and furious criticism - she has put on little weight since she was a teenager. Indeed, one of the rumours around her intense liking for the nose powder is that it keeps the pounds off - especially since the birth of her child. Thin is fashionable, and will be for a very long time yet.

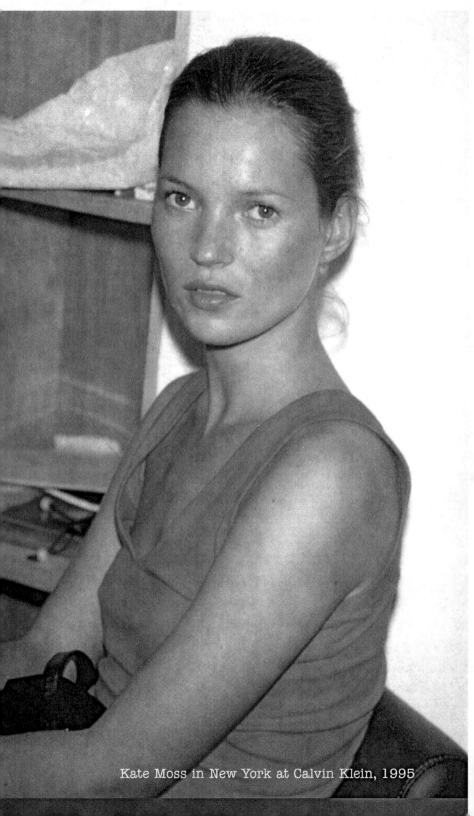

Kate Moss in New York at Calvin Klein, 1995

Kate Moss on a New York catwalk, 1996

Kate's big chance came about because of the emergence of the Style magazine in the '80s. These magazines, exemplarised by The Face and I-D, were aimed at creative youth and were different from the style supplements started in the '60s. These earlier versions lauded middle class values and the trendy hipsters who possessed mortgages, cork screws and cappuccino machines. '90s youths were barely interested in eating, never mind how to make a soufflé.

These style magazines coincided with the 'youth quake' in Seattle and Manchester that promoted a new kind of youth culture. The '70s had introduced Punk music, a violent, anarchic rebellion against the gentle, flaky '60s. Crowds of shouting, spitting, beer-swilling yobs replaced the gatherings of mellow hippies, a nightmare of crazed, unemployable youths piercing their bodies with safety pins. With its brutal, unrefined language, Punk was anti-poetic, anti-refinement and anti-human. But at least it was anti something. Nineties post-modern culture believed in nothing: nihilism and apathy rather than anarchy were becoming the defining statement of our time. It required different kinds of music and different kinds of drugs. Discontent centred on the soul rather than dissatisfaction with the state of the world. Belief systems were eroded and vanished.

On either side of the Atlantic there was one city in particular that cultivated this new attitude. They were twinned in spirit, if not materially. In the States it was Seattle, in England it was Manchester (the two are renowned for having the same weather: grey, dreary, rainy and utterly conducive to nihilistic misery). In Manchester, groups like The Stone Roses and The Happy Mondays gained a following from The Hacienda Club, fuelled by ecstasy and psychedelia. In Seattle, bands like Nirvana captured the bleak isolation and despair teenagers were feeling with their 1991 album Nevermind and the single 'Smells Like Teen Spirit'.

Grunge was born, a movement was based on jangling guitars and hard drugs. A listless war was waged against the soulless values of capitalism and the phoney glamour of material success. What the mood of the times craved was a new kind of reality, one that was truthful to the physical style of its adherents - Generation X kids whose parents had taken pills to avoid heroin but had slipped through the net, Slackers and New Agers on a diet of Grunge and Garage. This youth was unemployed, lived on sink estates and in squalid basement flats with fag ash on the carpet, damp on the walls, needles on the bedside cabinet and vomit in the bathroom - urban realism with its own version of truth and beauty. It glamorised self-destruction. Smack came right back into fashion.

Along with this new philosophy came a new kind of woman. Sick of manufactured, artificial beauties with no personalities, people wanted women who defined their era, women with whom they could identify. Not raucous punk princesses who lacked the edge but girls with attitude, like quirky American Chloe Sevigny, a street kid then model and actress who featured in Larry Clark's movie Kids, and English musician and muse Justine Frischmann of the band Elastica. What these two women possessed was a new elusive quality that defies description but was to become the watchword of the new movement. It was something about being able to gain acclaim and admiration without effort, individualism and a confidence in only the self that surpassed egotism and bordered on narcissism. Kate could embody that quality as well as anyone.

Kate had thrown herself headlong into her new role, though all this must have seemed pretty far off for an adolescent model at the turn of the decade. Initially, her jobs were few and far between, more of a diversion from the monotony of life than a career. For a year after she left school (with just one 'C' at GCSE) a lot of her work was unpaid. Kate had to fight hard to keep going: her mother was getting impatient. Where was the jet set lifestyle, the glamour,

the parties, the celebrities dropping round for drinks?
'She kept asking me when I was going to start earning some
money,' said Kate, 'and I'm trying to explain that you have
to do the editorial otherwise you'll be a catalogue girl for
the rest of your life. She didn't understand that I had to
do these pictures to earn money later.' As it happened, she
was right to wait for her opportunity. Tides were changing
in the fashion world and Kate was in just the right place
at the right time for a lot of people to make a killing –
herself included.

Because style magazines are iconoclastic they need icons
of their own, somebody who embodies what you are without
having to explain it. 'Show, don't tell' is the stuff of
drama, and so it was with the discovery of Kate Moss. Her
modelling jobs had produced portfolios, and photographers
used these to pick models for their magazine shoots. One day
a young woman saw a blurred Polaroid of Kate and decided she
encapsulated everything she was looking for. She was trying
to get work with The Face magazine and needed the right kind
of look. Kate was perfect.

THE FACE OF TOMORROW
Corinne Day was a former model who had graduated to the
other side of the lens. She liked skinny girls – she was
one herself. Corinne was a proponent of the grunge look and
Dirty Realism – photographing things as they are without the
use of artifice, mainly in shabby flats without expensive
clothes and props, a bit like the magazine wing of gimmick-

free filmmaking style Dogme. The approach was simple: you scoured the rails of Oxfam to find your fashion lines and didn't cover up the flaws in your models or the imperfections of your subject matter. Corinne had never planned on a career in fashion and, as with Kate's discovery at JFK, it was a chance meeting on a plane that led to modelling.

Also like Kate, Day had left school at sixteen with a minimum of education. Desperate to travel but without any money, she found work as a courier. A meeting with a photographer on one of her flights led to modelling work, and she embarked on a career as a fashion model. A boyfriend, New Zealand born photographer Mark Szaszy, taught her how to use a camera. For Corinne, though, photography meant purity and austerity, not the contrived beauty of make-up and careful posing. 'I wanted to instil some reality. I thought the girls I knew looked more beautiful sitting at home in their pyjamas than they did in Vogue. So I started just documenting them being themselves.'

Day's work was to be an example of photographic neo-realism, a hyper-truthful evocation of a generation that was stripped bare and attempted to capture this new bleak reality. It didn't have to be all ugliness. The American photographer Bruce Weber, although capturing the traditional beautiful people on a huge budget, had nevertheless started a trend. This was La Strada, set against a background of a new kind of post-war world, one brief moment in time when money didn't seem to matter.

The Face magazine, launched in 1980 by Nick Logan, was, like the other new grass-roots breed of style magazine, an arbiter of trends that covered the whole spectrum of pop culture - fashion, art, music, sport and celebrity. The Face reinvented magazines, producing new typefaces and zany graphics, and instigating a sort of hip new brand of gonzo journalism. Magazines like this one had little or no budget to glorify commercialism, no armies of stylists, make up artists, million-dollar photographers, fashion industry contracts or money obsessed, prima donna models. Instead, they simply improvised. In order to get started and keep cutting edge, journalists and photographers often worked for next to nothing, but a spread in The Face did more for your cred as an artist than any Vogue shoot ever could.

Day's photography, radical and democratic, was soon to capture a new bohemianism. When Phil Bicker, The Face's then art director, had wanted to find a girl who represented the spirit of the magazine, he found what he was looking for in Kate Moss - glorified by Day's art-without-the-artifice photography. 'She was completely against the whole modelling thing - very young and fresh,' he said. 'It just seemed right for the time.' It was natural, young and free, capturing exactly what was going on in England at the time. It wasn't '80s glamour: it was about the street. 'Everyone was saying, "Let's get off our tits and have a laugh. Be more real and not have to grow up so quickly and have fun",' Kate explained.

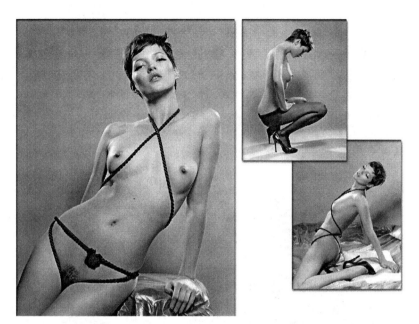

Not surprisingly, given the style of the magazine, it wasn't all glamour. Kate did one shoot for The Face when she was sent to the fabulous location of a tube station to model a T-shirt. She featured on her first cover in May 1990, clutching a football and wearing an Italia '90 scarf for photographer Mark Lebon (who, like many of the people she worked with early on, is still a friend). However, it was the July 1990 Third Summer of Love issue of the magazine that was to send ripples through the industry and constitute her first break.

During the summer holidays, Corinne took Kate to Camber Sands to do some beach shots. Kate, pubescent and skinny with all the hang-ups that go with a teenage girl and her body, went naked for some of the photos. 'I was quite shy, believe it or not,' said Kate. 'I was definitely more aware about my body, didn't want to take my clothes off. When I was fifteen, with Corinne, I cried and cried - I was so self-conscious! We used to fight all the time. Those shoots would take weeks and weeks. Nobody was getting paid.'

The agony paid off when Kate made The Face's cover for that July. In the photo Kate wears a toyshop-style Red Indian headdress. She grins, wrinkling her nose whilst squinting into the sun. The appeal is obvious: fun, natural, childlike, innocent.

'They styled me,' Kate remembered. 'It was completely contrived.' The slacker/grunge style was by Melanie Ward, who scoured flea markets and charity shops, partly to look unique but also because they couldn't afford anything more expensive. Inside the magazine, the young Kate is pictured running along the beach, in some shots hunched over to cover her breasts or using a straw hat to hide her crotch. It's early morning and the tide is way out; she looks freezing cold. 'I was just having a laugh,' remembers Kate. 'Corinne just wanted to bring out everything that I hated when I was fifteen. My bow legs, the mole on my breast, the way I laughed… I love those pictures, they're still some of my favourites even though I look so ugly in some of them. That topless one - my brother really caught it. All his mates going "I've seen your sister topless!" I can appreciate it now, it was a great picture. But at the time, I was like "Corinne, how could you give them that picture of me looking so gross with my flat tits!"'

Kate 16, Corrine Day

It was an exciting time for the two girls. For a short time, Kate even went to live with Corinne in London. 'We were really close friends. Corinne and Melanie and me would hang out all the time and talk about fashion and what we were going to do and draw pictures,' said Kate. 'Corinne had very strong opinions and very strong ideas about what she wanted to do. We did lots of the images that she wanted to do. And I think she did succeed in changing things a bit.' Looking back on the pictures it all seemed so simple, sweet and innocent, before everything turned on its head.

It was with Kate that Day would cement her idiosyncratic technique - shooting her subjects repeatedly, relaxed and unstyled, at home or in familiar, mundane settings. Her style was almost documentary, or even candid. It ushered in the era of grunge fashion. It was also the beginning of the 'waif' look that was so powerful and influential for so long. Playing on this aspect of Kate's physique was quite intentional. 'I think there was a bit of narcissism there because she was 5' 7" and skinny like me,' said Day. 'I'd been tortured at school for my shape and had a hard time for it as a model. I thought she'd had some of the problems I'd had and wanted to help.' Corinne's photos certainly did that, but at the same time Kate's rise to fame was coloured by the fallout of a global fashion scandal.

THE NAKED TRUTH

By the age of seventeen Kate had left Corinne's and was living in a west London flat with other up-and-coming fashionistas, like the photographer Mark Lebon. In late 1992, Corinne arrived at Kate's flat, commissioned by British Vogue's Alexandra Shulman to do an underwear shoot for the January 1993 edition. 'I liked the way she photographed femininity,' said Shulman. 'And her arrival on the scene coincided with a shift in the mood of fashion at the time. I loved the pictures and it never entered my head that there would be an outcry.'

On her website, Corinne writes an apology of the episode: 'I bought some underwear from Ann Summers sex shop in Brewer

Street which is where I live. I also bought some American tan tights, I got Liza Bruce to copy some T-shirts of mine so there were some designer credits in the magazine. The photographs looked cheap and tacky - everything that Vogue was not supposed to be. Kate had had a fight with her boyfriend that day and was crying so a few of the photographs were naturally sad.'

'I thought these photographs were funny at the time, they certainly weren't the kind of photographs normally seen in Vogue.' She wasn't the only one to notice that. The press had a field day with the pictures, and Vogue immediately stopped working with Corinne. Corinne hadn't anticipated the industry's reaction to what they saw as an almost cheap-and-nasty-porn aspect of the pictures. Worse, Kate looked about twelve and was portrayed as a hollow-chested child-woman, looking painfully thin in underwear that appeared too big for her - reminiscent of Jodie Foster as teen-prostitute Iris in Taxi Driver, or Nabokov's Lolita, the pubescent nymphet lover of a middle-aged scholar. She wasn't wearing make up and the dingy flat looked like a squat.

The pictures caused a furore - headlines screamed that the they promoted anorexia, drug taking and even child sex abuse. 'If I had a daughter who looked like that I would take her to see a doctor,' wrote Marcelle d'Argy Smith, editor of Cosmo UK. Other writers said they were a paedophiliac fantasy - which bemused Day and Kate. Kate protested:

'The whole paedophilia thing shocked me. I didn't know what people were going on about. I was eighteen, not twelve.'

Corinne was stunned at her pictures' reception, too, though she recognised another motivation in the harsh criticism she had to deal with. 'I was shocked when American Vogue ran my pictures next to Larry Clark's of real people, really strung out on smack, and called them the same thing,' says Day. 'Of course, grunge, being about Oxfam and not needing money to look cool, was no good for advertisers. Grunge never sold a £1,000 dress. I think they pushed the drugs label to see off grunge.'

As a result, Day was frozen out by the fashion industry and – more significantly – Kate was advised not to associate with her. It was damaging her career and, as it looked like Kate was about to take off big time, those in power realised that an association with this movement would kill off their golden gooseling.

Corinne and Kate parted ways and were only reunited in 2001. Corinne clearly felt betrayed by her former best friend. 'I was hurt by Kate,' she said in 2003, two years after seeing Kate again for a Vogue shoot in Blackpool. They hadn't spoken in all that time, and Kate had stopped crediting Corinne for her rise to stardom. All the same, Day says the reunion in Blackpool was 'like we'd seen each other only yesterday - she's the same giggly girl, very happy go-lucky. I always have a laugh with her.'

All the while, Sarah Doukas had been nurturing her discovery. She was - and still is - protective of her charge. Signs of interest had started to cross the Atlantic since The Face and Vogue shoots, but Doukas had to be careful to shelter Kate from harm. Young girls are vulnerable in the world of modelling to the predatory and unscrupulous characters that inhabit the fashion industry - not to mention such ubiquitous hazards as drugs and eating disorders. 'The most vulnerable time is the bloody shows,' said Doukas. 'That's why I hardly ever send young girls to Milan. I'm terrified of the place. I made sure Kate was chaperoned in the beginning.'

OBSESSION

For a while, it seemed unlikely that the fashion world could accept this new girl who was so determinedly anti-supermodel. After all, she was five foot seven - under height for shoots, never mind the catwalks - with snaggly teeth, bony bow legs and a skinny body, bearing a passing resemblance to The Lord of the Rings' Gollum: the absolute antithesis of the Lindas, Cindys, Tatianas, Helenas and Christys on Mount Olympus. Sarah Doukas initially struggled to get Kate overseas representation. One agency told her to come back 'when she grew into her face.'

The man to play the odds was Paul Rowland, founder of Women Management in New York and Storm's New York representative. There were big bucks in modelling and Rowland wanted to be there, but he had a wider vision of beauty than the traditional definitions. He loved Kate's look and knew that the pendulum was swinging in her favour: glitz, glamour, fake breasts, big hair and perfection were going out of fashion, in tune with the changing times. Kate's type was coming in.

Rowland asked Kate over to New York and she went, accompanied by her boyfriend of the time, American Mario Sorrenti, a former model turned photographer who had also worked for The Face. The pair had met when they both worked on a Wella campaign. Asking to photograph Kate had been Mario's pick up line and they had started a passionate and intense relationship. When they went to the States, their affair would eventually catapult them to fame. Kate lived in New York with Mario and his family - his mother Francesca, his brother Davide and his sister Vandida.

In the meantime, Kate's next big hit was a high-profile fashion shoot in America's Harper's Bazaar, edited by Brit Liz Tilberis. Kate would appear over no less than eight consecutive editions of the newly relaunched magazine, giving her enormous and invaluable exposure. Amongst those to sit up and take notice was Calvin Klein.

'She has this childlike, womanlike thing that I haven't

see for a long time,' said the King of Casual. 'It's a new kind of beauty. Not the big, sporty, superwoman type, but glamour which is more sensitive, more fragile.' Kate was booked for the next series of Klein's clothes ads and came under consideration to become the face of Calvin Klein - something which would be a stupendous coup and would launch her globally. The inchoate superstar busied herself with other work until she found herself with a six-figure Calvin Klein contract that precluded her from working for other brands but meant she could still do catwalk shows and magazine editorials. She represented Calvin's multiple lines for women's wear, lingerie and jeans.

The same kind of trouble seemed to follow Kate around during the early years of her career. Like Corinne's ill-fated Vogue shoot, the Obsession advertising campaign became legendary - not only for its artistic content but for the outcry it caused. When Kate appeared on the cover of Harper's Bazaar, photographed by Mario Sorrenti, Calvin Klein loved the combination and hired Sorrenti to photograph Kate for his perfume ads. He sent them to an isolated Caribbean Island, Jost Van Dyke. What came out of that trip was a ground-breaking hot, sweaty, sensual tour-de-force that has been copied and imitated many times since, but never equalled. Klein once commented on his ads to Vogue, 'I'm always taboo breaking. I've done everything I could do in a provocative sense without getting arrested.' He had always eroticised his advertisements, and this time excelled himself.

Klein had been trying to revamp the company's image, which had been stuck in an '80s groove since Brooke Shields, another baby doll, had spearheaded his jeans campaign with the tag line 'Nothing comes between me and my Calvin's'. Sales were falling and Klein was desperate to come up with a new look, something or someone who could capture the zeitgeist and relaunch his company as a global brand. Fabien Baron, the former art director of Italian Vogue had seen Kate's photograph and decided she was perfect for the new Calvin Klein ad campaign. He cast her alongside Mark Wahlberg (of boy band New Kids On The Block fame). Wahlberg's urban muscularity and machismo contrasted perfectly with Kate's fragility and innocence. Patrick Demarchelier photographed them in Calvin's underwear. The two weren't exactly captivated by one another. 'I like a bit more meat on my women,' said Wahlberg. Kate retorted she liked her men with more meat, too, although she did voice a complaint:

'My tits weren't big enough.'

The campaign included billboard and magazine ads, and then progressed to television. These advertisements were aimed at MTV and were not shown on terrestrial TV - they were considered too suggestive.

When Kate was shot on her own, most of the photos were nudes. One in particular features her lying on her stomach on a sofa, gazing up at the camera as if to say: 'Is this what you want me to do?' Unfortunately, Kate once again looks like a pre-teen and some inevitably accused

Klein of sexualising children. Critics said she looked like a vulnerable and compliant child. The photographs upset many people, who said they glorified her vacant face and emaciated, matchstick figure, thereby promoting anorexia, child pornography and violence. It was a slightly tenuous chain of reasoning. Nevertheless, women's groups got in a lather. The ads were targeted by the Boston-based Boycott Anorexic Marketing. Kate was compared to a 'kid from a latter-day Fagin's kitchen.' In some cities, anti-starvation graffiti appeared scrawled over the posters with slogans like 'feed me' and 'give me a cheeseburger', or a skull drawn over her face.

Kate was vehemently defensive. 'It was upsetting, absolutely,' she said. 'I was a scapegoat. The media had to put the responsibility on somebody and I was chosen. Just because someone is thin it doesn't mean they're anorexic. And no matter that I say over and over again that I'm not anorexic, they don't want to hear it. They're blaming me for a disease I have no control over.' The Heroin Chic debate wasn't far behind. The New York Times began, 'some social critics see an allusion to hard drugs in Moss's dead-eyed, hollow cheeked look.' As the heroin chic movement and its critics gained momentum, even pre-Monica Bill Clinton weighed in against the artistic use of the drugged-out look.

'You do not need to glamorise addiction to sell clothes,' he said, in the same characteristic drawl and rhythm that he would later use to deny carnal relations with the White

House intern. 'Some fashion leaders are admitting flat-out that images projected in fashion photos in the last few years have made heroin addiction seem glamorous and sexy and cool. And as some of the people in those images start to die now, it's become obvious that is not true. The glorification of heroin is not creative, it's destructive. It's not beautiful, it is ugly. And this is not about art, it's about life and death. And glorifying death is not good for society.' The fact is that it worked: the sickly, morbid glamour of heroin chic appeared in many Calvin Klein ads and undoubtedly played a large part in their success.

Kate's youthful love affair with Mario Sorrenti was a rite of passage for both of them. Although Mario was naturally blamed for making Kate a heroin-chic goddess, their relationship put them both on the global fashion map – he as a photographer, she as one of the most photographed women in the world. They were part of the tight little group of innovators - among them Corinne Day, David Sims, Juergen Teller and Glen Luchford - who changed fashion photography forever. The bubble burst in February 1997 when Mario's brother Davide, also a renowned photographer, died from a heroin overdose at the age of twenty. The horrible irony of this was not lost on the media - Kate and Mario had been seen to be glorifying heroin use and it seemed to justify all the arguments against them. Amy Spindler of the New York Times, who coined the phrase 'heroin chic', wrote an article attacking what she perceived as the evil of this fashion movement, accusing Kate and her circle of complicity. Davide's death hastened the end of the controversial style.

The point was driven home by a photograph that Spindler printed with her article. Jaime King, then a young model and later actress who starred in Pearl Harbour, was Davide's girlfriend and a recovering addict herself. The photo, taken by Davide, showed her sprawled on her bed surrounded by pictures of dead drug victims like Sid Vicious, Kurt Cobain and The Grateful Dead. The fashion industry's response was to close ranks; Kate and her kind became the scapegoats. But - like more recent drug scandals - the controversy did her no lasting harm. Some said it even earned her money.

'I suppose there was a moment when people were taking pictures that could give the impression of glamorising drugs,' said Mario Sorrenti in 2002 at an exhibition of his photographs. 'But it was very fleeting and the press made it

seem more significant than it was. Davide was just part of
the whole thing because he was there at the time. The main
protagonists were a slightly older generation. And it wasn't
just fashion. It was in music and art.' His contradictions
belie the fact that, although short-lived, heroin chic was
highly influential.

It was perhaps inevitable that Kate would be drawn into
this scene, as these people were the only ones she was
associating with at the time. Life was exciting and she
was young and impressionable. Even before the 'heroin chic'
movement, Kate and Mario found themselves very much in
demand. 'When we went to New York we were famous within
a year,' said Mario, now married with two children. Kate's
feet have never touched the ground since, so it is easy to
understand that she has never had time for a reality check.
'It was pretty insane,' says Mario about their joint rise to
fame. 'A whole lot of responsibility and a whole lot of work.
We were together for two and a half years and then we went
our separate ways. We're still very close.'

The Obsession advertisements brought her relationship with
Mario to a close. 'We fought all the time,' she remembered.
The couple were obsessed with each other, but the pressure
of the work and being together all the time brought their
problems to a head. Sorrenti insisted that Kate go naked and
wear no make-up for photo shoots. 'Mario was like "You have
to be naked man, it's about purity" and I'm like "what's the
difference if I have a pair of knickers on?"'

At the time, the pair also shot some film that was used in commercials. Jost Van Dyke looks eerie and isolated and the couple seem trapped with each other for all eternity. The black and white footage is raw, bleak, arty and disturbing; Mario whispers a voice-over proclaiming to Kate 'I love you, I love you', over and over again.

Mario may not have loved Kate forever, but everyone else would. His photographs sealed her reputation as the Waif, the label that would launch her into the stratosphere and is associated with her to this day.

Isaac Mizrah Fashion Show, Spring 1995, New York

4. In the Depp end

Kate Moss, Dazed and Confused Magazine, 1999:

My Mum used to say to me: 'You can't have fun all the time Kate.'

And I used to say: 'Why not? Why the fuck can't I have fun all the time?'

The first thing to say is that ladies, even if their mothers don't mind, do not use four-letter words to them. The second thing to say is that Kate's troubles with men and her incoherent lifestyle probably have their roots in her childhood, when her restless mother Linda left safe Peter Moss for bad boy Geoff Collman. When Kate did opt for security with caring, reliable publisher Jefferson Hack, the relationship failed - despite them having a daughter together. As the fragile, teenage waif, she sought out excitement with wild men... and for twenty years until she met Jamie Hince she kept doing it.

As a young star, living the rock'n'roll life and hanging out with the kind of men that go with it was practically mandatory. But as she was still doing it in her mid-30s, even her friends were raising eyebrows. A list of her past romantic attachments or one night stands is a Who's Who of the dysfunctional and off-beat: Sean Penn, Freddie Windsor, Lenny Kravitz, Liam Gallagher, Jesse Wood and Massive Attack's Robert Del Naja - to name only a handful. And that is only the men. Some of the women are equally unstable. Jamie Hince only seems a departure from the mean because against the likes of Doherty he appears a model of propriety. But he is not your average mother's dream son-on-law and, at forty and without any money, hardly a catch either.

JOHNNY DEPP

After she and Mario broke up, Kate didn't have to wait too long for another man to come along. Many, including Kate herself, say that Depp was the love of her life. 'I don't think I've got over my relationship with Johnny Depp,' she confessed in the aforementioned interview with Dazed and Confused Magazine in 1999. What was especially poignant about her comment was the interviewer would become the father of her daughter and only child.

Kate and Johnny met in 1994 at the Café Tabac in New York. There was chemistry between them right from the start. Johnny loved Kate's English accent. 'I was never in love with anyone until I met Kate,' he was soon heard to say. The pair started living with each other almost immediately. 'I'm crazy about her,' exclaimed Depp, later tempering his ecstasy to 'We're just having fun, a lot of fun.' At the time, maybe that's all that Depp wanted, though it was obvious that Kate was after more.

When the couple signed in at a hotel she wrote Kate Moss Depp. Johnny was not best pleased and told her to quit it.

Years after their break-up he said, 'Kate is somebody I care about deeply. But I wasn't very good for her at the time. She's better off without me.' It's true: at the time, Depp was almost as wild as Kate was when she was with Doherty. There

were certainly stormy times between them, the most famous
being in 1996 when Depp trashed a hotel room in New York
in a drunken rage, ending up getting arrested and having
to pay £7,500 in damages. After he was released he went
straight out to trawl some of New York's seedier nightclubs
and strip joints. He admits to having had an alcohol problem
in those days, using drink to dull the madness of his rise
from nobody to overnight star. Kate was the comparatively
sane one in the relationship, while Depp took drugs, boozed
and regularly attacked the paparazzi (a role that Pete
Doherty was later to take on with relish).

For all the tension, it's plain that Kate and Johnny cared
about each other very much. 'I bought these for my little
Kate,' Depp said in an interview in Premier magazine in
1995. He was on the set of his movie Dead Man, directed by
Jim Jarmusch. He showed his purchases to the interviewer.
They were skeleton necklaces accessorised with long strands
of copper, silver and gold beads. 'They were', wrote Holly
Millea, 'heavy, cold yet sensuous to the touch. Around
Moss's neck they'll warm to body temperature.' It is hard not
to recognise the irony of a man buying skeleton necklaces
for his girlfriend, especially if she happens to be the
woman accused of promoting the trend for skeletal figures.
Certainly Depp has - before and after Moss - shown a certain
liking for the gamine look, perhaps because that is how he
perceives himself: a man-child, a male waif, a Peter Pan,
vulnerable and exposed.

With Johnny Depp in New York at the premiere in 1994 of
Serial Mom

For her 21st birthday party in January 1995 Depp, who owns the infamous Viper Club in Los Angeles - where River Phoenix took a fatal overdose - threw a surprise birthday party for her there. Gloria Gaynor sang 'I Will Survive' for Kate who *'whore'* a long red satin dress. Depp took the scissors to it as they were walking out of the door, cutting it off at

Johnny Depp and Kate Moss shopping in Chelsea, 1995

the knee so the hem was all jagged. It was 'very Kate', as the fashion people say when describing something that is very sexy, very cool, and so of the moment that everything else looks passé. Depp was more mindful of the fact that his handiwork gave him a cue for punning 'wore' and 'whore'.

Depp certainly matched Kate in partying and willful behaviour. He was ten years older than her, had been married at twenty then engaged (to Winona Rider) but he was starting to think about settling down. And it looked like Kate wasn't The One. Perhaps he saw too much of himself in her, or realised she was too young and volatile for the stable family life he craved. 'I want to have children, I'd really like to be a parent now, but finding the right woman to share that with is proving difficult,' he confessed.

This may account for the indecent haste with which Kate was replaced: the vacancy was almost immediately filled by French actress and Kate look-alike Vanessa Paradis. She and Depp had two children in quick succession. No wonder Kate was heartbroken. Yet in 1995 Johnny had swooned, 'I can see myself being married to Kate for 50 years.'

By way of explanation for their split, Depp was content to blame himself, admitting he didn't give Kate the attention she deserved. In May 1998 he told the New York Daily News, 'Kate is somebody I care about deeply. We were together for four years, and she's a great, lovely, sweet, pure girl, really a great kid, and I care about her. I love her on a very deep, profound level. Distance is very difficult when you're trying to maintain a relationship, when you're thousands of miles apart for a lot of time.'

They were having too many fights and the long separations required by their respective professions were a huge pressure.

'I was an horrific pain in the butt to live with,' he said afterwards. 'I can be a total moron at times. I let my work get in the way which made me difficult to get along with.'

He says he cried for a week after they split up in 1998, admitting that he was - briefly - scared he that would never find another girlfriend to replace her. Kate, on the other hand, had convinced herself that Johnny merely wanted a break and that he would come back to her. She was besotted with Depp, and just couldn't handle the thought that it was over for good. When she finally accepted it, the realisation sent her into a spiral of drink and drugs that landed her in rehab in November of the same year. (On the day she left, Johnny gave her a $100,000 BMW as a gift.)

'There's something about him that she found utterly compelling. Everyone else has been a pale imitation,' said a friend. It wouldn't be until 2005 that another charismatic and troubled man would come along who would bowl Kate over and bring her to the brink of ruin.

In 2002, one of the Moss posse commented:

'We all have one love in our lives and Johnny was Kate's.'

This was before she met Pete Doherty, whom some say has usurped the Hollywood actor's place as her lost love. Until

Doherty's arrival, Depp was her obsession. In fact, some see Kate's enduring infatuation with Doherty as her way of replacing Depp and trying to relive the all-consuming love she experienced with the actor. In July 2005, The Sunday Mirror magazine featured the headline 'Is Kate still down in the Depps? While Johnny soars, his old flame sinks. Will she ever stop carrying a torch?' The feature inside covered the years since they parted in 1998, comparing and contrasting the lives of both. The article emphasised that, whilst the once-hellraising actor had now calmed down and grown up, his ex-girlfriend's life and behaviour had been going in the opposite direction – and that was even before the cocaine bust hit the headlines.

Her post-Depp spell in rehab in November 1998 was blamed on 'excessive partying', 'exhaustion' and 'depression': PR-speak for paying the dues of a rock'n'roll lifestyle. 'In fashion, excess is not for creative purposes, it's escapism,' Kate explained. A diet of champagne, vodka and drugs is the only way she could cope with the vacuous world of fashion, she maintained. 'It was the only way you could go out night after night and do those boring dinners. You're working all day and yet you still have to look like you're having a really good time. You're never allowed to be tired – it's a sin.'

Yet, Kate took to it all like a duck to water – it's all she knew, and she didn't even want anything different. Like a Titanic looking for an iceberg, she wasn't going to stop until she wrecked herself... and perhaps not even then.

Overseas Trips

When the coke bust hit The Mirror's headlines in 2005, it was
a catalyst for all sorts of other stories and storytellers
to come crawling out of the woodwork. Since the dam had well
and truly been broken, there was no point in maintaining
the vow of silence. The damage had been done and, after all
in its aftermath, there was money to be made.

Gavin Maselle, Storm's representative in South Africa, told
the story of Kate and Naomi Campbell's trip there in 1998

for a Versace charity fashion show organised by Campbell in aid of the Nelson Mandela Children's Fund. The pair were to meet Nelson Mandela himself. The tale unfolded in The Sun over two days of exclusive interviews in July 2006.

Maselle said he had known Kate for eight years, and that every time he saw her she was on coke. 'Kate has been addicted for years,' he told The Sun. 'I truly hope she stays off the coke because if she ever goes back, it will be the end of her.' This apocalyptic warning was accompanied by some pretty colourful stories about the high times they'd had, although even Kate would be hard put to sustain the prodigious intake of Class A drugs that his accounts routinely attribute to her. Doubtless Gavin twigged early on in his snort'n'tell negotiations that the more drugs Kate took the bigger his payolla.

In one irreverent anecdote - given Mandela's near-canonisation - Gavin described how Kate yanked him into the toilets just before they were going to be introduced to the great man, chopping out a line of cocaine and snorting it from the toilet seat. 'She was insatiable, I just couldn't believe what I was seeing,' he said. 'We were there at Mandela's house in the Bishop's Court area of Cape Town - and Kate was doing coke.'

On those trips, he said, Kate needed a line every five minutes. He estimated she must have spent over £500,000 on the drug. The evening before, Kate had partied hard and had passed out after consuming the date rape drug Rohypnol, along with more cocaine. Once, Gavin arrived at the Table Bay Hotel where Kate was staying to find a massive party in full swing. He claimed:

'Kate obtained five grams of coke, snorted the lot and passed out for hours.'

Gavin, who is gay, stayed the night with her to make sure she was OK. He told The Sun how Kate woke up with only one hour to go before their meeting with Mandela. Kate ran for the shower, asking Gavin to join her. 'So I stripped off and jumped in,' he said. 'I will probably be the envy of every straight man in the world. But it was one of those innocent things between friends.'

The next day was the launch of Storm Models in South Africa at Cape Town's Velodrome Stadium, which Gavin helped to organise. Kate had to have a line just ten minutes before the start of the event. 'She was running around backstage looking for somewhere to do coke.' She pulled Maselle into the toilets again and couldn't find anywhere to chop up her lines. 'So she just said, "Fuck it, the ground, let's do it off the ground." The cocaine was thrown on the floor, not even chopped up and divided into two. Then she bent over, bum in the air and snorted half in just one go.' He didn't mention what happened to his half. But from being an unmentionable where drugs were concerned Kate was now someone about whom skanks like Gavin could invent whatever could be printed.

Another episode of the same story chronicled Kate's relaxed attitude towards her sexuality under the influence of charlie. After consuming massive amounts of coke - 'these huge rocks of the stuff just in big thick lines. I don't even know how Kate got it up her nose, but she snorted lines of it' - Naomi and Kate slipped between the sheets together of the king size bed in her room. 'Coke can make

you sexually adventurous to say the least, sometimes even depraved,' said Gavin - a revealing choice of words given his own orientation. In fact, it points to these being descriptions made by a 'source' who is prepared to put his name to anything that the tabloid hacks think their readers will buy.

But he continues, 'I was in the suite and Kate and this American girl were clearly very interested in each other. We all ended up lying on Naomi's bed. Naomi was being very dramatic. She would go into the bathroom, snort, come out and change into this fabulous Pucci kaftan and rant and rave about her fabulous life,' Gavin told The Sun. The next day, he claims that Kate telephoned him to fill him in on who did what to whom. Of course, Naomi Campbell is another exposed junkie whom the Gavins can attribute exactly what the tabloids like to print without fear of redress.

These sources have it that Kate's day will start late, as she never gets to bed before 4 a.m. On waking up, she'll reach into her bag on the bedside table and rummage for a plastic bag of coke. She'll snort a line as a wakeup call. Then she'll pad downstairs, pour herself a glass of white wine. As the day wears on she'll drink champagne - Krug or Cristal - and then plan the evening's entertainment: what party she's going to attend, spending a lot of time on what she is going to wear.

Another source of tales is fashion PA Rebecca White, who reveals that Kate is known as 'The Conjurer' in her circle because of the expert way she handles

Kate at the 1994 book launch of
Naomi Campbell's *Swan*. Of course,
Naomi had not even read it.

cocaine. Kate also takes Ecstasy, Rohypnol and Valium, which Maselle discloses she carried everywhere in an ornate £65,00 Fabergé egg.

According to White, she drinks heavily to take the edge off the coke - otherwise she would be far too wired. 'Kate always wants to do drugs until they have all gone. Kate would never leave anything on the table.' White has also known Kate for years and said that Kate began getting heavily into coke again because she was worried about getting fat. She goes into rehab to 'rest' from drugs - not come off them completely. 'Kate does not want to come off drugs,' White believes. 'She doesn't want to be cured. She is in a frenzy. Every now and then she'll have a rest, but only so that she can go back on another drugs binge again with a vengeance. You don't invite Kate to a party if you don't want drugs there.'

A BED OF PRIMROSES

'Kate's philosophy is to live fast and if you want to do something you do it,' says one source.

'With Kate that doesn't mean trying your hand

at painting or climbing the Himalayas. It means having sex with whoever you want to have sex with, having as many drugs as you want to have and as much champagne and vodka. Anyone who frowns on that is just square in her eyes.'

Of course, the classic text of this philosophy is *to live fast, die young and leave a good looking corpse.* Kate is surrounded by friends and hangers-on who would never dare to tell her that is where she could be heading. Outside that inner circle, many say that Kate is bad news and that she is damaged, even though she appears to have rehabilitated herself so well. 'The general view is that Kate behaves in this way because, deep down, she is a very troubled person. She is really a lost soul,' says a friend. 'She is damaged and out of control. She has everything a woman can want, but it's not enough. She seems to seek out destruction.'

BOHEMIAN BABYLON
The Primrose Hill set had coalesced in '90s in the arty

enclave just north of Regents Park where a beau monde group of hard-living celebrities - pop stars, actors, fashionistas plus the requisite liggers who orbit the stars like planets - had settled or, in the liggers case, hung out. Jude Law, who lived there with his wife Sadie Frost, dubbed a female subset, which revolved around Kate Moss, of which his wife was one, the Moss Posse.

In the wake of the cocaine scoop, Kate's circle of intimates were flushed out and, in the ensuing bidding war, some sold or, at least, leaked their stories to the tabloids. It transpired that the heady cocktail of fame, money, drugs and sex in the Primrose Hill set had led to a veritable Bohemian Babylon of which the Posse was at the heart of the action. Orgies, wife swaps, threesomes and drug and alcohol abuse were everyday occurrences in the lives of these young, go-getting pleasure seekers. The cast of characters in this rock'n'rolla constituted [exposé, scandal, too much cocaine and the natural aging processes have all contributed to its demise] a veritable Who's Who of Cool Britannia.

Naturally, the Cocaine Kate scandal meant that celebrity hacks descended on the Posse like anthropologists would a Stone Age tribe discovered in the Amazon basin. There was, it seems, a pecking order in the inner circle, but with Kate as the ringmaster: 'ruthless, immoral, controlling and manipulative', who likes to play sex- and mind-games with the participants. To date, her meddling has been chronicled as accounting for the break up of nine couples.

The Posse - Kate's 'Disciples' - consists of people like Sadie Frost, ex-husband Jude Law and, after they split, her toyboy lover Jackson Scott. Pearl Lowe and her husband Danny Goffey of the pop group Supergrass are intimates. Pearl and Danny, Jude and Sadie were famously exposed as wife-swappers in a News of the World scoop in 2005. Female disciples are Stella McCartney, Naomi Campbell, edgy actress Samantha Morton, Brit installation artist Sam Taylor Wood, ex-Hollyoaks starlet Davinia Taylor, used-looking Meg Matthews (ex-wife of Oasis star Noel Gallagher, who seems to have ditched his old friends) and legendary Matron of Honour Anita Pallenberg, giving the circle some historical rock chick cred.

Patsy Kensit used to be part of the set but is now a clean, hard-working actress and mother of two sons, and wants nothing to do with it. Other members of the posse include Notting Hill star actor Rhys Ifans, rock star Bobby Gillespie, Anna Friel, party organiser Fran Cutler, Ronnie Wood and his family (Kate dated his son Jesse), Jade Jagger, Dan Macmillan, socialite Annabel Nielsen and Daniel Craig.

Just one of Kate's many highly publicised flings was the one she had with millionaire socialite and 'It' boy Dan Macmillan, who was seeing Jade Jagger at the time. Macmillan, heir to the publishing empire, the Earl of Stockton and grandson of British Prime Minister Harold Macmillan, was also a famous model himself, with a male waif look that had landed him on the front of Vogue Homme, The Face and others.

Some Posse, including Pallenberg, Lowe, McCartney...

Back in 1997, while Kate's relationship with Johnny Depp was on the rocks, she briefly poached the millionaire catwalk star from Jade - with whom Kate had spent holidays in Ibiza. Jade, who had hoped to marry Dan, her 'Vulgar Viscount', was furious and fell out spectacularly with Kate. Jagger is a jewellery designer and she sent Kate a name necklace with the word SLAG written on it. Jade and Dan broke up, and Jade moved on to other men. After years of avoiding each other, she and Kate have now patched up their differences after a chance meeting during another holiday on Ibiza.

Turning Over a New Leaf

MacMillan wasn't Kate's last fling with the publishing world. Following her final, cataclysmic break-up with Johnny Depp in 1998, as she slowly put the pieces back together after a spell in rehab, she was interviewed by a serious journalist named Jefferson Hack. She still wasn't over Depp. 'There's been a lot of different men mentioned in your life recently,' Jefferson Hack asked her, 'but no one permanent relationship... Is there no one out there good enough for you?' He was referring to the string of brief affairs she'd had since Depp and rehab.

'It's hard for me to think about being in love with anyone else,' she replied. The interview was the first time the two had met, not long since Kate left the Priory rehab clinic after suffering from 'exhaustion'. Some see Kate's meeting and subsequent relationship with Hack as a reaction to her state of mind at the time. She was at a low ebb, heartbroken over Depp and scared stiff of the consequences of an increasingly debauched lifestyle. After the roller-coaster ride of Depp and flings with others like him, Hack was a completely different challenge. She took him into her life.

Jefferson, who had long been obsessed with Kate, seemed to offer her some stability, calming down her party-going nature. 'He used to be sweet and nerdy, all specs and spots and developing crushes on beautiful models,' says one fashion journalist who knew both of them. 'Now, he puts himself about as the coolest thing in town. Behind his back, though, we all refer to him these days as Mr Moss.' Jefferson, who had worshipped Kate from afar when he was a student at the London College of Printing, fell madly in love with her.

When Kate met him, she was becoming increasingly desperate to have a baby. Jefferson was stable, down to earth, intelligent and dependable: ideal father material. 'I think she loves Jeff because he is straightforward, laid back, reliable and knows so many things,' Teresa Hack, Jefferson's mother, told the Daily Mail in 2002. She added:

'Jeff will look after her and be faithful, I am sure. He's had two or three girlfriends but he's not a womaniser. I know she has had some problems, but Kate is marvellously well now and they are so happy. She knows she can rely on him – nothing is more important to a woman.'

For a while, Kate seemed to have given up her party-girl lifestyle for the opportunity of settling down to have a family. Teresa remembers the promising start to the relationship. 'Jeff was so excited and I said to him: "This is wonderful as long as you make her happy and you love her." 'He replied: "I do, I do love her, I really do love her."'

In fact, Hack was a lot like Kate's father Peter Moss: solid, reliable, unfailing. He was sane and dependable – not as exciting as some of the characters she had been out with in the past, but a man who could provide what she needed and would never let her or their daughter down. However, just like her mother Linda's reaction to many years of reliable but unexciting marriage, sane and dependable was just not enough for her. Bad boys are just another one of her addictions.

Hack cared deeply for Kate, and still does, but he didn't have the fire that she craves in a relationship; he calmed

Kate Moss with Jefferson Hack at the premiere of *Artificial Intelligence* in New York, June 2001

her down for a while and was there for her at a time when she was extremely vulnerable, but ultimately, it wasn't in his nature to provide the excitement, drama and high jinks she thrives on.

FAMILY VALUES

'Everyone seems to be having babies at the moment.' The Primrose Hill set included plenty of mothers and babies in its ranks and Kate was getting broody. 'If I haven't met Mr Right in a few years, I'm going to do it anyway,' she had maintained in the past. She even considered turning to IVF if necessary, although in the event it wasn't needed. Early in 2002, she brought a pregnancy test home from the chemists and it confirmed what she had suspected.

She and Jefferson waited until the 12-week scan came through clear before they announced the news to their friends and to the world. Two weeks later the official statement was released after rampant tabloid speculation about the baby's name: 'In response to numerous press inquiries, Kate Moss and Jefferson Hack are pleased to announce that their beautiful baby daughter is to be called Lila Grace.'

Some aspects of the pregnancy weren't easy, particularly for a supermodel. Initially Kate resisted buying maternity clothes, until it became clear that hipsters just weren't cut out for this kind of use and she caved in to Kaftans. The change in shape obviously didn't go down too badly: in February 2005, a nude portrait of a pregnant Kate Moss

Well into her pregnancy, Kate on a shoot on the Millennium Bridge

by Lucian Freud sold for nearly £4 million. Kate herself
suggested both the project and the full-frontal pose. Lucian,
who is the grandson of Sigmund Freud, is said to claim droit
de seigneur from all his sitters. (Not the Queen, surely?)

Then, of course, there was her infamous 'party lifestyle':
pregnancy would mean having to curb some of her more
destructive habits - alcohol, drugs and cigarettes. 'Kate is
known as a heavy smoker, but now she is pregnant, things are
different,' her publicist claimed. 'I am quite sure she is
following doctor's orders and trying to give up - and if she
can't she will have been cutting down drastically.' But Kate
was still spotted months into the pregnancy, puffing away
with her mates, including Bobby Gillespie, with whom she would
soon be romantically linked in the celebrity rumour-mill.

The Primal Scream frontman, like Kate, had enjoyed more than
his fair share of vices. 'We all had bad heroin addictions
around 1994, and the band more or less ceased to exist,'
Gillespie told the Sunday Mirror. 'I was coming out of a bad
period. I was on the edge of psychosis. It's private, but I
had a really bad time mentally and I damaged myself badly
through a variety of drugs. It was so bad in 1995 that I
wasn't sure if I was ever going to make records again, and
that's what I love doing most.'

Kate and Bobby had worked on music projects together -
including a remake of Lee Hazelwood and Nancy Sinatra's
1967 duet Some Velvet Morning in 2002. They were spending

a lot of time with each other, to the detriment of their other relationships. Some said Kate had got what she wanted from Jefferson Hack and was now ready to start back where she left off, pregnant or otherwise. Katie England, Bobby's fiancée, was particularly unimpressed - the couple had recently had a son themselves. Katie was scared that she was going to lose Bobby to Kate: she felt that she just couldn't compete with a supermodel.

'When Kate and Bobby spend late nights and boozy days together, it gives people ideas - and it has been noted that they seem to be hanging out more than just good mates should. They have grown close and we've noticed that there is chemistry between them,' an insider told the Mirror. 'Bobby's totally rock'n'roll, which means people gossip about what he gets up to. Katie knows this but she's still worried. After all, Mossy is one of the world's most gorgeous women and what red-blooded man wouldn't want to be seen with her by his side?' Even, apparently, when she was well into her second trimester with another man's child. Jefferson must have felt she was slipping through his fingers.

There were long conversations between Kate and Bobby over the phone, and they were spotted holding hands on the way out of a pub, fuelling speculation that their relationship was about more than just music. Not surprisingly, there were rumours that Kate's child was not Jefferson's. All was denied.

Lila was born on September 29th, 2002, weighing 6½ pounds. For a while, it looked like Jefferson had won everything. Lila looked so much like him that there was no doubt who the father was. Almost as encouragingly, Kate appeared to be seriously considering giving up her high-octane career for a quieter family life. 'I can't do that Paris-London-Milan cycle any more,' she said. 'I got tired of feeling like Dracula. I wanted to see some daylight, and not just at six o'clock in the morning.' But it wouldn't be long before she changed her mind, seduced back into the party life by her close friend Sadie Frost, who had recently split with husband Jude Law. The days of Kate and Jeff were numbered.

Jefferson is the person who seems to have come off the worse from his intimacy and continued proximity to Kate. 'He has really suffered from his association with Kate,' a friend told The Mail on Sunday. 'She continually humiliated

Kate with Lila in January 2003

him, when he was nothing but nice to her. He really wanted to marry her.' Cruelly dubbed 'the sperm donor' and 'the babysitter' by Kate's friends, he was generally regarded by them and Kate at her many parties as a sort of hired help, fulfilling duties such as serving drinks. 'Rather than take part, he would only watch the proceedings with an attentive yet disinterested air, rather like a butler at a banquet,' wrote journalist Natalie Clarke.

Although there was no question of paternity, in the end a father to her child is all that Jeff would be to Kate. Friends say that she treated him 'like a PA, and would taunt him when she went off with other lovers. She could be quite nasty and spiteful. He wasn't into all her shenanigans and just wanted a proper relationship. But she made it abundantly clear she wasn't interested.'

'He also wants another child but Kate has been less keen,' a friend said. They never seemed like they were in love or had a proper relationship - at least on Kate's part. She treated him more like an assistant.'

Another source claims that the breaking point came when Jefferson walked in on Kate and another woman in bed together at his parents' house.

That must have made it abundantly clear that Kate was not cut out to be Mrs Hack, sober wife and mother to an eminently 'safe and boring' magazine editor.

'She sees herself as a free spirit,' said a friend whilst they were still together. 'And had never had any intention of committing to Jefferson for life and certainly not getting married.' Jefferson, by contrast, had become keener to marry as time went on - and increasingly frustrated by Kate's repeated knock-backs. 'I wish people would stop going on about it,' she often said when asked about their wedding plans.

In early 2004, while they were still together, she crushingly told a group of press and friends – in front of Jefferson – that she had 'absolutely no plans to get married.'

When the inevitable happened and their on-off relationship ended for good in March 2004, Kate made sure she got custody of her daughter. She also took pains to ensure that Jefferson wasn't tempted to salve his bitterness by accepting a kiss'n'tell offer.

As journalist Katie Nicholl of the Daily Mail discovered she actually paid an astonishing £2 million for the assurance, buying him a £1 million London property near her own house, along with a further £1 million 'goodwill' payment.

'They are going to have an amicable co-parenting situation,' a friend maintained. 'She wants to make it as easy as possible for them as a family. Jefferson's key demand was full and regular access and Kate has no problem with that. He will be able to see Lila as often as he wants and will have her to stay every other weekend.'

Then, the standard party line in these circumstances: 'Kate and Jefferson remain friends.' But what reason could there possibly be for a seven-figure payout? 'Kate is being incredibly generous to Jefferson because she loves him very much. She is just not in love with him,' the friend continued, but another source hit the nail on the head. 'Kate wants to make sure Lila is brought up somewhere nice with all the comforts she is used to.

She has also paid Jefferson a sum and, at Kate's request, he is to sign a gagging clause which means he will never be

Daniel Craig and his current girlfriend, Satsuki Mitchell, arriving in 2007 at St. Mary's Undercroft Church Westmister for the christening of Sam Taylor Wood and Jay Joplin's daughter, Jesse. Despite Sam being a member of the Posse, Kate was not invited.

allowed to talk about their relationship in public.' A cool £2 million richer for his silence, Hack finally accepted that what he believed was the love of his life never was and never would be. He loves Lila that little bit more for his unrequited love affair with Kate.

HACKED OFF

After the split Kate took up partying again. Daniel Craig became the short-lived object of her attentions in 2004. Craig had recently broken up with his long-term girlfriend, Love Actually actress Heike Makatsch. Fondly nicknamed 'Potato Head' by his friends, Daniel was briefly infatuated with Kate. She met him while he was making the film Enduring Love with her friends Samantha Morton and Rhys Ifans. There followed a romantic break in New York, where they holed up in a suite at the Maritime Hotel, and the pair later enjoyed a holiday in Goa along with Kate's mother, Kate's friend Sadie Frost and Sadie's then toyboy, Jackson Scott, who also despite no one mentioning it happens to be a fabulous flamenco guitarist. Like so many of Kate's flings, it quickly fizzled out. This time, Daniel was the one to lose interest first, much to Kate's chagrin.

Her ploy to keep him interested included turning up unannounced and uninvited for the première of his film Layer Cake - which also starred Kate's prime usurper Sienna Miller - at The Electric Cinema in Notting Hill. Sienna was only six months away from having Craig herself to pay back

A burnt-out Kate attending the London premiere of
Layer Cake, September 2004

her fiancé Jude Law for bedding his nanny while engaged to her. Daniel showed no interest in either - especially, a noticeably wrecked looking Kate. He preferred to keep himself entertained by the harem of starlets who surrounded him all evening. 'It did seem rather desperate of her to randomly be there,' recorded The Mirror's source. 'She wasn't even invited to begin with. To her credit she didn't try to gatecrash the screening - which was a good job as there wasn't one spare seat in the cinema. Perhaps ringing Daniel up next time she fancies seeing him would be an easier option.'

Recent stories suggest that at least some of her flings over the years have been a result of large quantities of drink and drugs, with men who have shared her penchant for these. Lurid revelations in tabloid newspapers about the now notorious Primrose Hill Set confirm that she is adventurous in her sexual tastes, with threesomes and one night stands featuring high on her list of leisure activities. But as she gets older, Kate's behaviour seems to be getting more extreme - and, some have suggested, increasingly desperate. Cavorting round Glastonbury and tearing up the town with notorious wild boys maybe fine when you're eighteen; it starts to look unseemly when you're in your mid-30s.

There is probably some psychological significance in the way that most of her recent conquests tend to be much younger than her, and her targets (pre- and post-rehab) have demonstrated her continuing fascination for the sort of men more suitable for women ten years her junior.

Showbiz hacks on the tabloids mocked her for being an 'arch groupie', although this was little more than putting her down because they hadn't been able to stand up that she was a coke-head. The fact is from the beginning of her entry into the celebrity circuit she has hung out with rock'n'rollers.

BEAUTIFUL AND DAMNED

Amongst the faces in her inner circle, one character stands out: Marianne Faithfull, Kate's mentor. The legendary Faithfull is an infamous icon of pop folklore. She was Jagger's girlfriend, the girl in the fur rug (and, if you are of a culinary salacious disposition, Mars bar ingester) in the '60s Redlands drugs bust, a singer and movie star, a reformed heroin addict who lived on the streets for two years and finally, international personality. She was cast as the devil in a stage version of William Burrough's black fable The Dark Rider (it could be Faithfull herself) at the Barbican in 2004. Kate was there, of course, and proclaimed Faithfull as 'Brilliant, bloody brilliant.'

It has to be said, although some stories are too good not be true, that in 2007 when Marianne was tackled about the '60s Mars bar she said that she was still mortified by the rumour. She pointed out, 'I am very prudish. That is the real me. Maybe I was different when I was doing drugs and drink, but I wasn't **THAT** different.'

Marianne and Kate became an odd couple, going everywhere with each other. If there was a gallery opening, a fashion show or concert, Kate and Marianne would be there together. Marianne was guest of honour at the christening of Lila Grace in 2003 and sang 'I Get a Kick out of You' to Kate at her 30th birthday (which contains the line, 'Cocaine doesn't give me a kick…' - this would be ironic if Kate hadn't built up such a tolerance that it's practically true).

Kate seems to idolise the older woman. One year she hired a chauffeur driven car to bring Marianne down to Falmouth to spend Christmas with her and her family. She paid for her to fly first class to Jamaica to join her on a luxurious beach holiday. She buys her diamond earrings and other expensive gifts. Some say that in Marianne Kate sees something of herself: the baby, the lovers, the money squandered, the same heady sense of desperation, the eternal search for something more.

Marianne had Jagger and lost him. Kate had Depp and lost him. They are kindred spirits.

Someone close to Kate has said, 'Despite her outward show of arrogance, the disdain for friends and family which borders on, and sometimes transgresses downright rudeness, she is, at times, an insecure wreck.' Another noted, 'She likes to see herself as this wild, abandoned, carelessly free, rock-loving, party-giving, thrill-seeking girl of our times but privately wonders how it all happened and when it will go away. She is desperate to change but doesn't know how. Marianne is the real deal, a romantic legend, an incredibly intelligent, gifted woman; she is the daughter of a baroness and an extremely creative, fascinating being, a great survivor. Kate wants Marianne to tell her how to do it, how to become a legend.' There was also the fact that Marianne had been a long-term junkie but had kicked drugs.

Part of Marianne's personal brief seems to be educating Kate in the things she has found creatively important. Kate, after all, left school as early as she could and has little formal education. Amongst other things, Marianne encouraged her to read F. Scott Fitzgerald, thinking that the early 20th century American's novels of decadent glamour would resonate with Kate. One of Fitzgerald's books, The Beautiful and the

Damned, set in 1922, is a satire on the nouveau riche: 'a story of New York's nightlife, of rich, aspiring aesthetes and beautiful women, of ambition and squandered talent.' It caught Kate's imagination and, with romantic ambitions and characteristic enthusiasm, she decided to theme her 30th birthday party around it in January 2004.

Thirty is widely recognised to be a major milestone. The 'Return of Saturn' is often a time in life when people turn to introspection, assessing their lives and taking stock of where they are, what they have achieved and where they are headed. It can be a time of great insecurity if the three decades of life are found to be lacking. If Kate had any such existential angst, her preferred strategy for dealing with it was ruthless obliteration. The party turned out to be a decadent marathon that lasted 30 hours and was to become something of a cause célèbre.

One magazine called it 'one of the most shocking nights of debauchery ever seen in London.'

At the time, the lawyers made sure there could only be whispers about what actually went on, but after September 15th, 2005, Kate became fair game. The Daily Mail lost no time at all, chronicling the amazing goings on in an article published just days after the coke scandal broke. On paper, at least, the timetable looked like a fun-packed day:

12pm: Lunch at London's swish Mandarin Hotel with
Jefferson Hack, Sadie Frost, Stella McCartney and
Meg Matthews. Kate wears a canary yellow dress and
leopard print coat.

3pm: Back to her suite at Claridge's where she
greets guests and opens her presents. Among them were
Tiffany bags, gifts from Cartier, De Beers, Bulgari,
a £300,000 diamond necklace from Louis Vuitton, a
reported £15 million five-year contract from Calvin
Klein, 'a load of D&G stuff', a diamond encrusted
Agent Provocateur whip and undies and from Jefferson
Hack, a star named after her and £1000 telescope to
look at it. The party starts in earnest. 30lbs of
caviar is consumed and 30 cases of Cristal champagne
are drunk. Kate wears a blue sequin encrusted thirties
dress with matching cape.

9.30pm: On to the adjoining west London houses of Sam
Taylor Wood and Agent Provocateur owner Serena Reese
where at midnight two topless male models wheel in a
3' high profiterole birthday cake. She is serenaded by
Jools Holland and sings Summertime with him.

1.45am: Environmental Health officers are called to
the house after complaints about the noise.

3am: 50 remaining guests taxi back to where the
party continues.

Journalist Katie Nicholl of the Mail on Sunday viewed the party at first hand, putting her in a position to fill in some of the events that the timetable missed. One room at the Claridge's suite featured an orgy where everyone was invited. 'A tangle of bodies writhed on the king size bed. All I could see were limbs tangled in abandonment... a young woman appeared from behind the curtains and readjusted her dress strap, not noticing that her left breast was exposed. She sidled up to us, clearly inebriated, lipstick smeared across her mouth. 'Have you any condoms?" she asked.' This free-for-all was watched by Jefferson Hack 'with a look on his face which said that he'd seen all this before.'

Although there were drugs in abundance, Kate was very careful about being seen actually doing any. The other guests could do what they wanted, but she had a reputation to maintain - and there were too many guests around at this party for her to risk anything in public. 'Everyone knows Kate does drugs, but she does them privately,' a friend told Nicholl more recently. 'If it's just her and Pete and a couple of mates, she'll open a wrap and share it, but in a situation like her 30th where there were so many people, she wouldn't take the risk. Kate's not stupid. Why do you think she's been able to get away with this for so long?'

Looking back on it all, it is amazing that Kate managed to keep her secrets for so long. In the aftermath of her fall from grace, her previous life took on the appearance of a house of cards, a fragile construction kept standing by a combination of narcissistic bloody-mindedness, chutzpah, good luck and, when all else failed, litigation. The sheer scale and duration of her vices should have made them impossible to conceal. There were suspicions, of course, and there were rumours; some (like The Sunday Mirror) had even tried acting on good information and been stung by her lawyers for their trouble. No one touched the subject without getting burned. Perhaps the party lasted so long because Kate really was as careful as her friends say, and the exposé was just bad luck. Or perhaps she grew complacent after so long, thinking she was untouchable. Probably a little of both is true. But however careful she was, there was one factor that was always going to be out of her control, a chink in her seemingly impenetrable armour. Falling for Pete Doherty was the worst and, then, in one of those utterly unpredictable and unintended consequences, arguably the best thing for her career she has ever done.

I see paint-cracked walls stained
with shite
Long long lock-up days
Cold lonely nights
And I think to myself ...
what a wonderful world
I see men touching fists
Saying 'watcha bruv'
Screams from below
Shit parcels from above
And I think to myself...
I see my true love
On a Rimmel advert

RIMMEL

**PETE DOHERTY,
JANUARY 2006,
PRISON DIARIES.**

5. Cocaine Kate

THE SKANK

Pete Doherty was infamous long before he came into Kate's orbit. A former member of the cult rock band The Libertines, he was a notorious junkie with a heroin and crack cocaine habit. In 2004 he was sacked by the group for failing to address his increasingly disruptive addictions. Two years previously he had been jailed for two months for burgling his band mate Carl Barat's flat to buy drugs. After several failed attempts at rehab he agreed in early June to enter the Thamkrabok Monastery in Thailand. This majestic Buddhist temple (the name means 'Temple of the Bamboo Cave') has a fearsome reputation for its highly controversial but equally effective heroin rehab programme.

The Sun reported on his admission with almost sadistic delight: 'His mum, bandmates and even Libertines manager Alan McGee reckon his spell in the notorious hellhole, which nestles on a mountainside in Saraburi province, is his last chance. The tough "prison" is run by an ex-Marine who says: "The method of punishment is the bamboo stick."

'Gordon Baltimore, from Harlem and known as Phra Gordon, says: "For 30 days the patient is nothing but a robot. We push the button to decide when he eats and when he sleeps. Once someone starts his programme, the only way he can quit is when he's dead."'

Aside from being beaten with bamboo canes, the treatment also involved drinking herbal medicine that purged the system by causing vomiting. The amazing thing was that Pete lasted three whole days before doing a bunk one morning at half past four, fleeing to Bangkok where he went straight back on the smack before returning to Blighty.

Phra Gordon issued a statement: 'Having entered into the free treatment program at Thamkrabok Monastery in Thailand on June 10, and having vowed to senior monks "never to take drugs ever again" upon registration, Peter refused to take even his third dose of medication, and has finally today rejected the sensitive and compassionate care offered by the Nuns and the Monks there.' A condition of leaving the monastery was that he signed a declaration, which Phra Gordon claimed he did (at 4.30 a.m.!): 'Thamkrabok Monastery have done everything they could to help me, but I am just not strong enough for this treatment.'

When he returned to England from Thailand Pete was promptly arrested for possessing a flick knife and given a four month suspended jail sentence. Because of his son's habit of dropping out of rehab programmes, Pete's father said he was 'everything I most hate about humanity' and vowed not to lay eyes on his son again until he was free of drugs. The tabloids lapped up this real life junkie soap opera... and this was before he met Kate.

When Kate did meet him, Pete already had a boy, Estile, with a Lisa Moorish who, given she also had a daughter, Molly, with Oasis singer Liam Gallagher, was a genuine 'arch groupie'. Pete was everything Kate didn't need, especially as, however precariously it stood in the balance, she still had a reputation to lose. Kate being Kate though, she could no more resist a really dangerous bad boy with a minstrel's soul than she could a big fat line of the Bolivian marching powder.

A kind of Saint of the Damned, Pete had a loyal and obsessive posse of fans and hangers-on who, rather than helping him to beat his demons, vicariously lived out in morbid fascination his flirtation with death. For them, he represented the romantic fantasy of the doomed poet and self-destructive artist. Perhaps they wanted him to fulfil the destiny of other broken heroes like Jim Morrison, Kurt Cobain, Janis Joplin and Jimmy Hendrix, and end up as a dead monument to rock'n'roll excess.

But despite his permanently drug-hazed appearance, Pete knew exactly what he was doing - or at least, what he was getting into. Entering into the Byronic image was quite intentional, even if that kind of lifestyle tends to be rather trickier to leave. 'My dealer was always smoking roll ups and I asked, "Is that opium?"' he told the Sunday Mirror. 'I had a romantic vision of taking opium. I didn't think of it as smack.' Whilst the two of them played word games about definitions for varying types of narcotic, Pete set about the serious business of developing a really first-class heroin addiction that he knew with his not untalented musicianship would make him a star.

Kate would finally cross paths with her soul-mate and nemesis at her 31st birthday party on January 16th 2005. Whereas her last bash had been a Bacchanalian extravaganza, with activities not witnessed since the days of Caligula's court, her 31st was planned as a more 'low key' affair. Instead of Claridge's, it was held at her farmhouse in a small village in the Cotswolds, far away from inquisitive journalists and impertinent killjoys like Gwyneth Paltrow (who had been so shocked at the previous year's proceedings that she had taken one look before leaving early with her husband, Coldplay's frontman Chris Martin, firmly in hand).

Kate had bought the farmhouse expressly for the purpose of hosting her favoured kind of soirées. A property she had rented in the area for three years previously, Walnut Tree Cottage, had been the subject of legal proceedings after Kate had trashed the place so badly it resembled a junkies squat (which, of course, is precisely what it had been). Used as she was to a bit of debauched squalor, even she was shocked when she first saw the state of Pete's Shorditch pad.

The noisy, drug-fuelled parties at Walnut Tree Cottage, unlike those at Shorditch, had the neighbours up in arms, complaining about everything from the noise to Kate's guests crashing out on their lawns. The christening of Lila Grace had taken place there, and her daughter's inauguration to church life had turned into a boozy weekend marathon attended by 100 guests. The damage wrought to the cottage had cost £10,000 to repair. The inhabitants of the sleepy little village weren't happy country bunnies.

'The whole atmosphere of the place has changed,' one pensioner told the Sunday Mirror. 'I've been disturbed many times late at night by her parties.' The last straw was…

'She bought a drum kit last year and kept everyone up. This is a village where people come to enjoy the quiet life. It's not a place for the likes of her.'

There were fewer star birthday guests altogether in 2005. Many had decided to give it a miss, probably on the grounds that they were still recovering from the last one. There was no Janet Street Porter - Kate's 'intellectual friend', as she dubbed her - who had ended up knickerless on the floor with her legs in the air trying to join Kate on the bed. No Jade

Jagger, who was in Mexico. No Grace Jones. No Tracy Emin. No Stella McCartney, who was pregnant.

Most guests were the satellites of fashion - make-up artists, stylists, model agency staff and other lesser mortals. Of course, Sadie Frost was there with her boyfriend Jackson Scott, moaning about the fact that her estranged husband Jude Law had got engaged to Sienna Miller without telling her - a problem that would go away of its own accord, with a minimum of help from the tabloids in the form of his highly-publicised fling with the children's nanny. At Kate's 30th Sadie had made a spectacle of herself on leaving Claridge's with one breast 'none too perkily on show' for the benefit of the assembled paparazzi.

The theme for this bash was 'Rock and Roll Circus' - a reference to the film of a 1968 Rolling Stones event that had also starred Marianne Faithfull, amongst many others. The Sun newspaper had trumpeted the night by claiming, 'The party will be Kate's wildest ever.' It is uncertain how they expected her to live up to this promise. 'Last year was special but this year is taking things further. Everybody will be decked out in glam-rock outfits and booze will flow all night.' The barn at Kate's 17th century property had been decked out in red, yellow, black and white, in keeping with the cover of the Stones' album. At 8 p.m. the guests started to arrive in convoys of cars, the long driveway lit by tall flickering candles. One of the cars held the tousled, baby-faced and, likely as not, stoned figure of Pete Doherty.

Kate had always been close to rock groups since she began as a young model. She'd featured in pop videos, once appearing as a pole dancer in The White Stripes' I Just Don't Know What To Do With Myself. Pete had recently formed his own group, Babyshambles, and his producer was former Clash guitarist Mick Jones. Mick's wife Miranda was also a friend of Kate's and, given that Mick had been roped into doing a DJ spot at the birthday party, it was no surprise that he managed to wangle an invite for his protégé Pete. What was a surprise was that Kate spent most of the evening sitting in Pete's lap whispering sweet nothings. They spent the night together and announced they were a couple.

Kate's friends, her management and the press were just gobsmacked. Not because Pete would lead Kate astray - she was quite capable of doing that for herself - but because Pete's life was a circus. He was constantly surrounded by an entourage of fans, groupies, tabloid journalists, hangers-on and weird stalkers like Max Carlish (a sort of super-groupie and tyro film-maker who made an infamous movie of his relationship, or lack of it, with Doherty). It was also known that Pete would speak to anybody about anything for the right money, part of his expensive drug habit's survival strategy. So, for that matter, would his circle of hangers on; there was no honour among junkies in this group. How on earth was Kate to keep her mystique and her habits a secret with Doherty around? Moreover, how would it affect her role as a mother, as she tried to keep Lila Grace from becoming entangled in the life of her devil lover and his disciples?

But Kate and Pete weren't such an odd couple. Both were individualistic hedonists with addictive personalities who craved the next high; Kate saw in him something of the dangerous charisma she had worshipped in Johnny Depp. 'I know he's bad for me,' she once said, 'but I just can't help myself. There's something about him. I keep going back.' She described him to her friends as 'dangerous, exciting, creative and very talented.' And there is no doubt that Pete is talented and creative, a brilliant musician with a real flair for song writing. Like so many others, though, his genius seems to come at a price. Kate knew that Pete's first allegiance has always been to drugs. She once wrote in a verse:

'You love them [drugs] more than you love me/ So that's why I could cry all day/ That's why I can't breathe.'

Even though Kate is no saint herself, Pete's lifestyle was an undeniable mess and his problems were compounded by the sort of drugs he uses. Coke tends to produce a euphoric and energetic high (hence its status as drug of choice amongst hard-working models); in the case of heroin, the 'high' is accompanied by a strong depressant effect, relaxation and lethargy. Recently, the press have printed photographs of his squalid flat in east London, littered with the detritus of a chaotic, drug-centred existence. Moreover, Pete had made a

Faustian pact with the tabloids who were given 'anonymous'
accounts of his activities. In the months that followed, they
were treated to a blow-by-blow account of his and Kate's love
affair, even though it appeared that neither Kate nor Pete
had spoken to reporters.

Kiss'n'tell obviously runs in the family. Pete Doherty's
mother Jackie has recently written a book, Pete Doherty:
My Prodigal Son. In it she describes him as a 'sick and
fragile boy'. The book is full of desperate chases to
find her son before he succumbs to a sticky end. He is
constantly surrounded by fans and musicians so his mother
can never speak to him alone (a problem Kate has shared).
Kate's recent mission seems to be to get him away from this
entourage; whilst he is with them, she believes, he will
never be free of his habits. Jackie Doherty recounts how she
and her husband have fallen out many times over their son.
Jackie never switches off her mobile and will take calls
from him at three o'clock in the morning if she has to. This
has been the cause of serious friction with her husband, who
says Pete should be left to make his own choices.

Jackie agrees but will not let him down. 'You have to allow
people to live how they want to live,' she says. 'Because amid
the chaos is a creativity I don't understand.' Pete does not
seem to have a background which would explain his addiction.
The Doherty family provided a stable and conventional
upbringing for their poet son and two daughters. Peter
Doherty Senior is a major in the Royal Corps of Signals.

A prodigy from an early age, Pete was an insatiable reader who devoured Brecht, Baudelaire and the Romantic poets. He was obsessed with Oscar Wilde.

Jackie has only met Kate once. 'I think everyone should leave them alone,' she opined. 'They've been deeply in love and people just won't leave them alone.' Whilst she does not blame anyone but Pete for his addiction, she loathes some of the seedier members of his entourage. 'Pete is so trusting,' she says. 'But some of them steal from him.' They even, she claims, sold photographs of Pete to The Sun, taken as he was ostensibly injecting an unconscious girl with heroin. (Pete hit back at his tormentors, claiming that the photo was completely staged and that, in any case, he was drawing blood out with the girl's full consent, instead of injecting heroin while she was unconscious. He likes to paint with blood on occasion. The walls of his flat are daubed with messages written in his own blood.)

Jackie Doherty might be right in her view of her son as a misunderstood poet, a sensitive innocent abroad, overwhelmed by his emotions and talent, but Pete is all too often his own worst enemy. As the tabloids, gossip magazines, broadsheets and Kate's friends launched into attacks and why-o-why

pieces on the odd couple, Pete seemed only to encourage the
media frenzy that was becoming his life. He'd sold his 'My
drugs hell' story to most of the papers now and so, in order
to keep his source of income, he now started to sell stories
about his new love and muse. 'It's been the best week in a
long time because I've really found love,' he claimed. 'I
believe her when she says she loves me and I know I mean it
when I say I love her.'

It didn't help matters when he was pictured in the Sunday
Mirror a few weeks after meeting Kate smoking heroin, 'a
pathetic fool chasing the dragon'. Photos were provided by
Max Carlish, Doherty's twisted Boswell. Carlish was paid
£30,000 for them and then sold them again to the News of
the World. The paper used them as a very public warning to
Kate of what her boyfriend was up to - as if she needed
telling. She was more furious about the betrayal; it made
her realise that Pete's entourage were snakes in the grass
and that she'd better be careful.

Pete physically attacked Carlish for the betrayal, which
landed him in court on an assault charge and led to him
spending four nights in Pentonville. As part of his bail
conditions he was ordered into rehab. In order to pay for
it he sold the story to The Sun, the main thrust of which
was that he was doing everything for 'his angel Kate'.
Kate was naturally furious and precipitated the first of
their many break-ups, of which it would quickly become
impossible to keep track. The charges of assault on Carlish

were eventually dropped, but whilst Pete was in rehab some grainy pictures of him and Kate appeared in The Sun. Kate was furious and again dumped him, this time on Valentine's Day. They had only been going out for a month. Pete argued that his mobile phone had been stolen and the pictures sold by someone unknown. He counter-attacked by castigating his sweet angel for dumping him in his hour of need.

That kind of exchange would become the pattern for their on-again, off-again relationship. A few weeks later in March 2005, Kate was relaxing in a pub with Rhys Ifans when, off his face, Pete marched in and jealously confronted Kate. The slanging match ended with Ifans threatening Pete to 'just leave her alone'. Pete explained later, 'I'm a bit paranoid and insecure. But she's one of the most beautiful women in the world, so who wouldn't be insecure?' Given that regular crack users often manifest aggression, paranoia and delusions, his insecurity was more likely a side-affect of the pipe than fear of losing Kate.

Kate was certainly paranoid about her own image. She needed to keep up the fiction that she was as pure as the driven snow - she thought her career depended on it. Some cynics might say that if she were so concerned she wouldn't be associating with someone so incendiary. But, as she explained, she was hooked - his allure was as addictive to her as crack was to Pete. All she needed was to get Pete clean and they could become this legendary rock'n'roll poetic couple, a personality cult of epic proportions. Staying clean in her

Kate and Pete at the 2005 Glastonbury Festival. While he wears his trademark trilby, she is just a coke-jagged wreck.

mind meant him not smoking crack. Everything else was fine; Kate had no intention of giving up her own addictions - the fags, the booze and the coke. After all, she'd been handling those with minimal media fallout for years.

THE MEDIA FEEDING FRENZY

During the summer of 2005, Pete and Kate were the It Couple, the Sid and Nancy, Mick and Marianne, or Kurt Cobain and Courtney Love of the day. They swanned around the rock festivals looking wasted and unkempt (and were duly voted 'skankiest couple in England' by one gossip magazine) and were pictured in clubs crooning to each other. At Glastonbury they took part in a mock wedding ceremony at the chapel of 'Love and Loathing in Lost Vagueness.' They were kicked off a Mediterranean cruise because Pete was smoking crack dangerously near to the petrol tanks.

All these activities were said to be eroding Doherty's talent as the voice of a generation and he was accused of being the consort of an empty-headed clotheshorse. Critics complained that, whereas in the beginning Kate had inspired him to be more creative, she was now doing the opposite - sapping his creative juices and reducing him to the role of a sideshow. It was a great excuse for his lack of creative output, but Pete's track-record proved that he was more than capable of turning himself into a sideshow, if not a corpse.

Over those few months, Pete became more and more of a liability, getting flakier and more paranoid by the day. He was due to support Oasis in Paris in May, but never made it; he and Kate had a drunken, jealous punch-up on Eurostar and ended up going home. The carriage they were in was wrecked. Even then, though, Doherty was telling the world that he and Kate were in love. 'I love Kate very much,' he said. 'We're definitely going to get married. We are trying for a baby together.'

Whilst all this was going on Pete was also trying to complete Babyshambles' first album. Songs were in short supply and Pete's behaviour was so erratic that hardly any work was getting done. As fans and the pop world waited with baited breath for this magnum opus, Pete's record label Rough Trade insisted everything was going well. To prove it, a single entitled 'Fuck Forever' was released.

Some felt the proverb 'he should have a long spoon that sups with the devil' had never seemed more apt: Kate had made some enemies in the Doherty camp and the envy incited by her seemingly effortless wealth made her, in some of their eyes, fair game. Kate must have had a sense that one of Pete's disciples might betray them for the tabloid's thirty pieces of silver. (Most fingers point to James Mullord, Doherty's ex-manager, which The Mirror discounts.) The drugs sting in the studio, which took place during an evening recording some of the tracks for the first album, was really an inevitability waiting to happen. Impoverished skanks like like the Babyshambles set don't pass on a prize like this.

Kate and Pete were in New York when the scandal broke. Kate, as chronicled, was renowned in the world of fashion for her drugs use but the celebrity tabloids had failed dismally to stand it up. Nonetheless the more she sniffed at the white powder the more hacks there were sniffing around to expose her. Bingo: her number inevitably came up. One of Pete's friends within the nest of vipers had decided Kate Moss was too rich a prize to pass on out of respect (there is no loyalty among junkies) for the Albion minstrel. Kate was no longer immune from the curse of modern celebrity: ruinous tabloid exposure. Forever more she would be...

...Cocaine Kate.

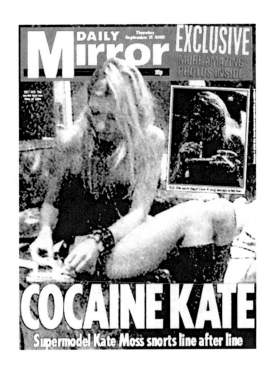

When it finally happened, Sarah Doukas - Kate's long-term agent - was charged with the touchy business of breaking the news to Kate. As her agent, much of the flak hit her. 'Look, Kate has always been an unbelievably private person,' Doukas told The Times. 'I've never seen the side of her that they've written about. She's always gone to work every day. You couldn't sustain an excruciating schedule if there was a serious problem. And her schedule has been really tough. The past three or four years there's been almost more business than I could deal with on my own, which is why I hired two more people to help. Of course, I read the papers, but I didn't believe most of it and I didn't feel it was my business to probe. I certainly wasn't going to say: "So, is it true about the three in a bed stories?" It's not my place to discuss those things.'

Tellingly, Doukas has always known when a story concerning one of her models has been about to hit the headlines. Not this time: the sting was carried out as carefully and secretively as 9/11.

The scandal signalled that Kate Moss's days as the Queen of the Night were over. The fortress had been blitzkrieged. She was no longer the cool party girl; she was now a junkie with a crack-head boyfriend. She had also incurred the wrath of the Mirror Group by suing them when they suggested a year earlier she had used Class A drugs. Now they had got their revenge. She was denounced as a hypocrite and a liar. Even Lila Grace was used in the anti-Moss propaganda.

'Kate, mother of a two-year-old daughter, has no qualms about being seen with illegal drugs.' This was an intimation that in the ensuing fallout she might lose custody of Lila. The Mirror group was playing hardball and from their perspective rightly so. Kate had sued and won on an issue that everyone on the inside knew she was liar and, in suing, a blatant cheat to boot.

The Mirror Group is a lot smaller than it used to be but it will always be bigger than KateMoss plc. Kate's hubris deserved what it looked like she was going to get... the irony was she not only didn't get it she also returned more than if her fall from her endorsement clotheshorse hadn't occurred.

But that is not the way she planned it – she just got lucky.

The Kate Moss party looked like it was about to end – suddenly, ignominiously, and finally. She was set to lose £4 million in advertising contracts. A furious H&M dropped her from their imminent campaign for the hot new Stella McCartney range, suggesting a domino effect could ensue – Chanel, Burberry and Rimmel would surely follow suit. The fashion and beauty industry was also minutely dissected and criticism heaped upon it as it was revealed that Kate's edgy playgirl image – such a danger to young women – was the very thing that had made her such a phenomenal success. The fashion industry had played on it up to the hilt.

KATE PLAYS POSSUM

It looked like curtains for Cocaine Kate, with prosecution and even imprisonment a possibility. On legal advice, she stayed stum and went to ground by going into rehab, staying in the £2000-per-night Arizona Meadows Clinic for a month. This stymied the Met police who wanted to interview her and, as the lawyers teased out the worst case scenario, the media began backing off from her 'use' of cocaine to her 'alleged' use of it. After all, what proof was there that the powder was cocaine?

The fashion industry didn't understand her legally-directed gambit. 'Some people thought it was a cynical move on her part,' was the take of one fashion insider. 'They thought she just did it so she could keep her contracts and get the press off her back, but it wasn't like that. She was doing it for herself, for her family and for Lila. The thought that she could lose her child really upset and frightened her. Her daughter is the most important thing in her life.'

Pete did not have a million-dollar career to protect. In contrast to Kate, his career and image seemed only to be enhanced by his drug addictions. It was expected, after all, of a tragic poet. For Pete himself there seemed no need for the dash to rehab; in any case, he had been in many times before and when faced with the choice and pain of giving up drugs he had always chosen to stay on them and pay their dues.

The problem for Kate was that if Pete wasn't off drugs, it tainted her image. She paid for him to go into Meadows, but he quit after three days, claiming he was bored. That was very awkward, as Pete was an integral part of her problem: how could she be seen as clean, resisting the considerable temptations presented by the fashion world, when the one person closest to her showed a complete lack of commitment to her and her struggle? As part of the process of rehabilitation, Kate had to distance herself from Pete. She was furious with him anyway. Within days, Kate had supposedly ended the relationship.

On his return to England, Pete was immediately arrested again for possession of crack cocaine. 'She shouted and screamed at me,' he told one journalist, with characteristic indiscretion, about Kate's reaction to him quitting rehab. 'She threw her mobile at the wall. She's furious. With the amount of coke Kate was taking, it's amazing she got through rehab. I don't know how she stuck through five weeks, because I was bored senseless.'

The spurned Pete was one of many people who had a pop at Kate's own reasons for going into the clinic. 'Everyone believes she went in there to beat her cocaine addiction,' he explained. 'That's wrong. She did it to save her career. Having said that, she came out saying it works. But she is terrified of her will-power failing. She's petrified of getting caught again. She knows if she ever went back to drugs she would have to be more discrete.'

The point that Pete didn't understand and probably still doesn't is that when the stakes are high enough Kate stops using, whereas there is nothing in Pete's life that is as important to him as his drugs. The simple verse Kate had penned contained more truth than anything Pete Doherty has ever written or sung:

> 'You love them [drugs] more than you love me/
> So that's why I could cry all day/
> That's why I can't breathe.'

Kate remained silent, other than making a brief statement of ostensible contrition, which was drafted by her lawyer, Gerrard Tyrell, to ensure that her expression of regret did not amount to an admission of guilt. There was still the threat of prosecution. After she left rehab, she stayed away from England - living in California and Europe for 142 days - before coming in to face the music. Sir Ian Blair, then

Commissioner of The Metropolitan Police, had made it clear he was out to make an example of Kate. Tyrell outplayed him: when his client came in the music was all from Kate's songsheet.

She flew into London from Paris where she had been working in February 2006 and, wearing a Prada trench coat, black hair band and dark sunglasses (a present from Sadie Frost) she reported to Wellington House in London where she was questioned for 90 minutes at the Met's Specialist Crimes Operations Headquarters about her drug use. After reading a prepared statement, she followed legal advice and refused to say anything beyond confirming her name and address. She was released without charge.

But that wasn't the end of her problems. With the Cocaine Kate headlines, a whole army of unedifying stories broke - tales of sex and drugs beyond a paparazzo's wildest dreams. Chief amongst them was the revelation of her bedroom antics with other women. Jefferson Hack, the father of her child, must have cringed when he saw the 'Cocaine Kate's

three in a bed Lesbian orgies' feature in the News of The World in September 2005. These stories had been bursting to come out and, after The Mirror drug exposé, the media could say what it liked about Kate Moss without fear of legal redress.

The lurid 'exclusive' recounted tales of Kate's rampant and uninhibited bisexual life, alleging a long-standing lesbian

Left: Kate with Jude Law at a rock concert in 2005. Meg Mathews above and left, between Jude and Kate at the same gig.

relationship with Sadie Frost and actress Davinia Taylor. The women had frequent threesomes at Davinia's home, Supernova Heights, which she bought from Oasis guitarist Noel Gallagher and his then wife Meg Matthews. Kate also had sex with Sadie and her then husband Jude Law. 'Kate is far more amorous when she's high and often makes the first move,' said fashion PA Rebecca White. 'She's OK about all Sadie's men but doesn't like Sadie sleeping with other women.' Kate's earlier stay in the Priory is credited for this development.

She is said to have emerged a lipstick lesbian, keen on the very feminine women who were a part of her world. It was the Sex and the City era and it became fashionable among her set of friends.

In the various breaks from her sporadic but ongoing relationship with Pete, she also played the male field for all it was worth, racking up quite a catalogue of conquests. At Christmas 2005, after she'd left rehab and dumped Pete for his betrayal, she invited a 20-year-old boy, Jamie Burke, to accompany her on a skiing holiday. She had met Burke, a friend of Richard Branson's son, on holiday on his island, Necker, and had been smitten with the handsome model and ex-public schoolboy. Doubtless in an effort to make Pete jealous, she informed all the newspapers and was seen with him constantly at her side on the slopes at Aspen, Colorado. Kate had apparently told friends: 'I want a lot of disposable men in 2006.' And in relation to Burke: 'Finally I'm having some fun.'

It was not so much fun for Jessie Leonard, Jamie's 23-year-old girlfriend, who told the press that she had just spent a lovely romantic Christmas with Burke, her boyfriend of 18 months. 'I didn't even know he'd met Kate Moss until I woke up on New Year's Day and put on the news,' she said. 'It flashed across the bottom of the screen: "Kate Moss in Aspen with new boyfriend Jamie. They met on Necker Island." When your trust has been betrayed it's shocking and awful.' Charterhouse-educated Jamie told Jessie he was 'flattered' by Moss's attentions. Jessie said: 'I know it would be hard to resist Kate Moss if you were a man. But the hard thing was we were very much in love when it happened.' The fling, however, was very short lived with Kate claiming, 'Jamie was an amazing lover, but nothing else clicked.'

Not all her plays were successful; she was rejected by Serge Pizzorno of Kasabian, who gave her the brush off for coming on too strong at him at a festival, accusing her of being desperate. He was certainly ungentlemanly in his comments to the press when it appeared she was back with Pete. 'That poor kid Pete Doherty is going to marry her,' he commented. 'All I can say is good luck to him. He can have her. Because otherwise I think she'll be looking for a man for the rest of her life.' A headline on the Daily Mirror's 3AM GIRLS screamed out that 'the question on everyone's lips in London these days is: Has Kate Moss lost her touch with men?'

Franz Ferdinand's Alex Kapranos also saw her off, calling her 'the new Patsy Kensit'. She did seem to fare rather better with Albert Hammond Jr. of The Strokes at a party to celebrate the group winning Best International Band at the NME awards in February 2006. 'Being with Kate was drunken and friendly. She's a cool girl and I had a fun night, but I'm seeing someone,' he later said. Another wild evening in New York saw her snogging tubby American novelty singer Har Mar Superstar, and she was spotted 'canoodling' with Jackass star Johnny Knoxville at a Franz Ferdinand gig, and then later on in London.

One of the more ill-advised of her recent amorous escapades
has to be her brief dalliance in May 2006 with the new
TV sensation, the whacky Pete Doherty of stand-up comedy,
Russell Brand. Brand, who resembles a Victorian pimp in
looks and speech, is a recovering junkie himself. ('The thing
about heroin,' he told Jonathan Ross, 'is that it's a bit
moreish'.) He unashamedly chases any skirt with a g-string
underneath it and makes no secret of his proclivities; in
short, he ticks all Kate's boxes. Always dressed in black,
tall and lanky with stove pipe legs, a tousled beehive of
black hair and a baby-doll face, Brand resembles the bad-boy
rockers she so adores. He is also smart: sexually Kate is
always upwardly mobile.

Brand, however, lacks so much as a shred of shame or
discretion. After he'd slept with Kate he immediately boasted
about it to the press. Kate was furious, not being used to
her conquests kissing and telling and treating her in such
a cavalier manner. In an interview, Russell said, 'As far as
I'm concerned, sex with celebs is a wonderful thing. There's
a certain glee to the act of having sex with someone and
thinking: "Hey! You used to be on telly and now you're in
my bedroom!"' She also hated the fact that he allegedly made
money out of the story: after the cocaine Kate set-up, she
was on red alert over anyone in her circle peddling stories
about her to the press. Rejection and ridicule from men was
something Kate had never experienced before, until now.

Kate's friends have said that her behaviour is something she knows is wrong but can't seem to help. 'She's very aware she is stuck in this cycle of destructive behaviour,' said one. 'She knows she chooses destructive relationships and she wants to change that. She's more like a predatory man than a woman when it comes to relationships. I think seeing her parents' marriage fail had a big effect on her. She finds it hard to commit because she saw this failure at such a young age.'

Another claimed, 'Kate's not happy being the eternal party girl and wants to get a bit more normality in life and one way of doing that is to try to get to the root of her problems.' Some think one of the roots of her problems is that she is still carrying a torch for Johnny Depp: after him, a recurrent theme of her liaisons with men has been a reckless, self-destructive excess that smacked of a flight rather than a coming to terms with her inner demons.

THE ONE!

Throughout the troubles and press frenzy that surrounded every aspect of her life since September 2005, it is clear that Kate maintained a genuine affection for Pete. Despite his betrayal and the repeated lapses into behaviour that was destructive for both of them, the splits were never permanent – although they were periodically inevitable given her anger at how he exploited their relationship to feed his habit and damaged her career with his inability to keep his drug use from the attention of either the media or the police.

Consequently, when they were together, Kate made sure they were rarely seen publicly, hoping to convince everyone that they were no longer a couple. Kate couldn't risk being seen with him until there was some evidence that he renounced drugs for good. 'When they split up, Kate was keen to be seen cutting off from him for the sake of her family,' said a friend. She also want to placate her mother, Linda, who would become incandescent at the very mention of his name. So Kate went about her business… partying, going on holiday, modelling; whilst Pete went about his… brawling, taking drugs, attending court, going in and out of prison.

Kate's friends kept telling her to get rid of Pete, but as time went on she just seemed more and more determined to stick with him - even though she had so much to lose by continuing the relationship. There were numerous hints at the possibility of an engagement, some by the celebrity-based press, some by Pete himself. 'He said they were planning a "special day" with close friends and something "magical" would happen that afternoon,' said a source. When Kate attended Bobby Gillespie's wedding in July she reportedly told friends, 'It's going to be me next!'

But a life of wedded bliss just didn't square with the reality of Pete's addictions. Until he got those under control, she knew there could be no future for them as a couple. Kate began to lose patience. She had stuck by him for a long time, but she wouldn't wait forever. He was going to have to make a choice.

The crunch came in the autumn of 2006 when Pete was summoned to court to answer five counts of possessing drugs including heroin, cocaine and cannabis. Some charges related to arrests back in April, though one referred to possession of crack cocaine as recently as August 7 2006. He pleaded guilty, but his lawyer argued that Pete had been making 'positive progress' in his fight against drugs. The judge at Thames Magistrates Court granted him conditional bail until September 4 on condition that he stay at a rehab clinic, the Priory in Roehampton, and observe a 10 p.m. to 8 a.m. curfew.

Pete escaped jail this time, but the shock of the bail conditions and the threat of losing Kate for good did enough to keep him in the Priory. Friends were amazed; it looked like the first real step toward rehabilitation he had made in years. 'We've heard him say he'll get clean a million times, but a lot of his attempts have been half-hearted,' said one. 'But he's shocked us all. The latest bout of treatment has worked wonders. He's had a new implant fitted to stop opiates having an effect and he's taking pride in his appearance. The motivation he needed was losing Kate. She is undoubtedly the love of his life.'

The future looked promising… but one swallow doth not a summer make. When it came to a final showdown between Kate and drugs in Pete's heart, drugs would always win.

Pete took to performing mock drop kicks
on the increasingly bold paparazzi

6. Putrid Pete

It is obvious that Pete appealed to Kate on more than one level. He is bright, articulate and highly creative, and his self-evident intellect and musical talent are qualities she found utterly compelling. Undoubtedly his love for the 'party-lifestyle' was initially a part of the allure too, although the appeal of that eventually started to pale - partly due to the coke scandal, but also due to the growing realisation that Pete was losing his battle with addiction and could expect to be pushing up daises, well in his case opium poppies, if he didn't turn things around soon. The problem was that Pete seemed incapable of taking control or responsibility for his life. Given the state of the 'mates' who surround him, that only left Kate.

Early in October 2006, she was forced to take matters into her own hands. On leaving the Priory, Pete had immediately begun a tour with Babyshambles. His diary, published on a blog site, suggested that things were indeed looking up. 'Things are most certainly taking a turn for the... well, better? Compared to last tour's absolute carnage and freefall oblivion the first of the pipeless frog gigs and I can actually remember it.' Writing in something that has more in common with Nadsat, the teenage argot of Anthony Burgess's A Clockwork Orange, than with modern English, he later confessed that he was staying clean for Kate's sake.

'No palming stones off scallies in alleys, not with the missus here anyway.'

After spending two days with him in Ireland, Kate returned home to London whilst Pete got on with the tour. But, without the watchful eye of 'the missus', he could palm all the stones off scallies in alleys he wanted - which, as night follows day, he did.

One of Kate's friends allegedly told the Mirror, 'Pete deliberately didn't take drugs in front of Kate when she was with him in Ireland. He promised her he wasn't taking anything and she was so proud of him. But the night before she left, Pete told Kate he had to nip away from her to make a phone call. Instead he nipped to the local chemist for some syringes.' She didn't find out until she got back home. When she heard, she was absolutely livid. 'She was screaming at him down the phone, calling him all sorts. One of his bandmates heard her scream at him: 'You're so fucking stupid. I thought we were working through this but you're not going to change. If you don't sort yourself out everything's off.'

In the next days of the tour, The Mirror records that Pete spent in the region of £500 per day on crack and marijuana (thanks to the implant, his heroin days are over). As Babyshambles continued their line-up in England, matters came to a head. At three o'clock one morning, after a raging argument about his drug habit, Kate threw him out of her house, after which he was spotted roaming the streets, barefoot and forlorn, until he regained the presence of mind to go to his agent's house.

Kate didn't leave it at that. A few hours later she picked him up and issued him with her final demands: either he quit the tour or he lost her for good. Pete buckled. The official reason given for the cancellation of the remaining tour dates – just two hours before the next gig, in Liverpool – was 'artist's exhaustion' but it was really Kate's ultimatum. EMI, Pete's record company, released a statement: 'Babyshambles have made the decision to postpone the remaining five dates of their UK tour. It has become clear that Peter embarked on the arduous and high-profile tour too soon after his discharge and still needs time to recover from his extensive rehab treatment.'

'That was the moment Kate won,' a source told The Mirror about the ultimatum. 'Pete accepted the only way to save their romance was to call off the tour. There's no way Kate will put up with Pete lying to her. She is madly in love with him but, at the same time, she is no fool. When they aren't together Kate phones Pete about twenty times a day - because she is besotted. But she's also determined to hold on to the love of her life and she wants his baby now. That is the stick she has used to persuade him to come off tour.'

Leaving the fallout of the cancelled tour behind them, Kate and Pete travelled up to her Cotswolds farmhouse where she spent the next two days trying to talk him around. She was so concerned about his habit that she hired a bodyguard to stop any of Pete's drug-dealer mates from getting anywhere near them.

'Kate is so determined to help Pete kick the habit she's more or less locked him up in her home where he's safe from any bad influences,' a friend of hers told The Mirror. 'She wanted him to breathe the fresh air and realise that it is possible to appreciate the nicer things in life without having to resort to drugs. She really wants to make a go of things with him, but they can't do this while he is on those substances. She knows it is hard, but she is begging him to do it for her.'

There was an ulterior motive for this act of desperation. Kate had reached the end of her patience with Pete's wayward ways. She had a future to think about, and she wanted it to be with him, but his addiction currently made that impossible. 'I love him and know that for all his faults, I will spend the rest of my life with him,' a friend quoted her to The Mirror. 'I want my little girl Lila to have a brother or a sister. But Pete has to stay off the drugs. And the only way for that to happen is if he's with me all the time.' The source continued, 'Kate has never felt so confident or sorted in her career. Ironically she's become more of an icon than ever since she fought her own drugs battle and she feels ready for another child. She doesn't want the age gap between Lila and her sister or brother to be too great. But she's a bright woman and she wants Pete to be clean - she knows she can't have a baby while he's still into crack. That's why she is so determined he should ditch the tour.'

Kate and Pete's Endgame

Kate continued to police Pete's drug habit but even when he wasn't with the band the flat of his was like an opium den. She began a campaign to move him into her town house in St John's Wood, but even when he was finally evicted from his own flat he resisted. He told friends that he didn't like the idea of being 'under surveillance by the drug squad'. He embellished, 'Sometimes when I use the loo there I wonder if she has had a secret camera installed.'

His own eviction was in September 2005 - actually while he was doing a stint of rehab in the Priory - over a little matter of £10,000 of unpaid rent. His landlord, Andreas Panayiotou, called him the worst tenant he had ever had:

'Apart from the owed rent, the walls were smeared with blood and decorated with graffiti, the floor was carpeted with broken glass and used syringes and fungi were growing underneath the speakers.'

Kate knew that having Pete in her home was the only way to keep him where she could ensure he kept to his drug rehab programme and stayed away from his drug-infested circle of friends. There are other reasons focusing her mind on trying to make it work with Pete. Once upon a time she was young and carefree, and so were her friends. But life has a way of sneaking up on you. A lot of people wake up one morning and realise their youth has disappeared, only to be replaced by a mortgage, steady job, partner and 2.4 kids. That wasn't true of Kate but her damage limitation exercise over the Cocaine Kate exposé had made her think about her future. A lot of her old partying Primrose Hill set were also starting to live the grown-up life. In their own special and idiosyncratic ways, they were settling down into something approximating families and having kids and putting down roots.

She had deliberately chosen to have a child with Jefferson Hack some four years previously but had not seriously thought about settling down with him. He had repeatedly asked her to marry him, especially after the birth of their child, but she hadn't been ready for the stable family life. It wasn't her: it wasn't rock'n'roll, it wasn't exciting enough. She had turned him down many times before finally making the permanent break.

He had stayed around for a long time, and not just because the couple had a daughter together. He really cared about her, and watching her go through a high-profile list of celebrity relationships after their own relationship ended must have been agony. Many people think that he was waiting for her to come round and get back together with him. And, for just a short time, it seemed like she was going to. Two years after the split, around Christmas 2004, the couple were reported to be 'set to give their romance another go'. It had never been a particularly clean break, what with living so close together, sharing the same circle of friends, having joint custody of Lila and, frequently, romantic dinners together. Jefferson could be forgiven for getting mixed messages about it all; Kate even told him that, had she not met anyone else, she would like Jeff to be the father of her next child. Now, briefly, he seemed to have got what he always wanted.

The business with Daniel Craig heavily underscored that Jeff and Kate weren't destined to be together after all. This time, he got the message loud and clear. He moved on. In October 2006, Jeff had got engaged. His fiancée was another supermodel: 24-year-old Belgian catwalk sensation Anouck Lepere. Another supermodel, fully eight years younger than Kate and in the absolute prime of her career, marrying the father of her child? Ouch. It probably doesn't help that, unlike Kate, Anouck was highly educated, had studied architecture before she became a model. Jefferson has never been the party animal that Kate is, and now he has completely tired of that kind of lifestyle. Like so many of her other friends who lived it up, Jeff had settled down, enjoying an evening in on the sofa more than a night out on the tiles. Kate was becoming a rare breed in her age group.

There was also the example of the only real soulmate up to Pete she'd ever had: Johnny Depp. He had also moved on: taking up with Vanessa Paradis, whom he met filming The Ninth Gate in 1998, so soon after dumping Kate. They had stayed together and now had two children: a daughter, Rose, age seven, and four-year-old Jack. Indeed, Depp, despite his reservations about marriage as a ceremony was rumoured to be making it legal with Vanessa. This from a man who always maintained that 'if you are together and you love each other and are good to each other, make babies and all that, for all intents and purposes you are married.'

The Daily Express had recently reported: 'Johnny and Vanessa are planning to finally get married next summer at their villa. It will be a private event rather than a showbiz extravaganza. They are deeply connected but the children have made them really close. They're happier and more in love than most married couples.'

'Kate still finds it difficult when she sees pictures of Johnny and Vanessa arriving at premières holding hands,' a friend told the Daily Mail. Indeed, Kate seems never to have got over that break-up. 'She used to say there was something about him that was utterly compelling. There's no doubt in my mind that he was her great love,' continued the source. There is also no doubt about getting him back, though: that ship has sailed.

Back in 2004, when Jefferson and Kate looked set to make another go of things, a friend, in a Daily Mail article, made a penetrating analysis of why the editor of the Dazed and Confused magazine appealed to her. It was something she had taken on board during her relationship with Johnny Depp and has never forgotten:

'Johnny once said to Kate that if you're not particularly clever or cultured yourself – and with the best will in the world, Kate is not a Mensa candidate – then you

should surround yourself with people who are. Kate thought that was very good advice and has operated on it ever since.'

Jefferson fell squarely into that category - though the image was tempered with his media-friendly persona and popularity with the Primrose Hill set. Jeff was the best of both worlds. 'He's hugely creative and intelligent - he was a grammar school boy - and when Kate met him she was immediately impressed by his brain, as well as by the fact that he appeared completely unimpressed by who she was.'

This is precisely the appeal of her mentor, Marianne Faithfull, and exactly the same could be said of Pete. For all his problems with drugs and run-ins with the law, there is no question that Doherty is an extremely intelligent, gifted musician. A straight-A student, his career as a talented lyricist began at the age of sixteen, when he won a poetry competition and subsequently toured Russia on a trip organised by the British Council. He cites Wilde, Baudelaire and Huxley as just a few of his influences (not to mention the Romantic poets who also sparked his interest in 'opium'), and his songs are peppered with literary and philosophical allusions. She made her mind up to seriously try for the last time to make it work with Pete.

A very serious Kate, in July 2008, en route to collecting an AWOL Pete

Towards the end of 2006, Kate was snapped wearing a chunky antique diamond ring. Having finally confirmed their engagement publicly, rumours about the wedding were rife. Christmas or January 16th, Kate's 33rd birthday, were suggested. Friends claimed that they would probably head to Ibiza or Jamaica to tie the knot and continue Pete's rehab. 'They don't want a big, fancy wedding. Both of them just want to run away somewhere no one will find them - that's why Kate thinks Jamaica will be perfect,' one source maintained. (Just how perfect Jamaica might be for a recovering addict is another question.) Others claimed London's Marylebone Registry Office would be the location: close to home and the site of many of their friends and musical idols' weddings. Pete even bought her a second-hand Christian Dior wedding dress for the occasion. It cost him £120.

Whenever the date, whatever the location, whatever the outfit, Kate finally looked set to tie the knot. After two years of a roller-coaster relationship with Britain's most infamous musician, the most famous model in the world was ready to settle down. Pete was one addiction she was not prepared to give up: his addiction would give her up.

Meanwhile, the old advertising maxim that 'there is no such thing as bad publicity' was beginning to trump the Cocaine Kate debacle. Her career was picking up stronger than ever. After a brief dip in popularity as retailers jumped ship in the knee-jerk reaction to the coke scandal, they came back stronger than ever. The predicted and expected Armageddon did not happened. In fact, advertisers were clamouring and paying more for a piece of her.

Scandal sells. Kate was already a regular in the pages of the tabloids; everyone knew her, which is why she made such good advertising material in the first place. Following the bust, there were suddenly a whole lot more column inches, all absolutely free of charge. Kate had been outed by The Mirror for snorting charlie, a global scoop that triggered a publicity tsunami that was as big as the Clinton-Lewinsky scandal but this uneducated, uncultured greengrocer's daughter from Croydon did not crack up, get herself arrested or, more importantly, make an exhibition of herself. She kept her dignity and, most of all, she stayed cool. This was in mark contrast to Pete's performance. Hers didn't go unnoticed either by the public or the players in the fashion world.

The derailed Kate Moss train was back on track. Ads must first get noticed before they can sell product – Kate now had noticeability and, not least, respect in spades. Storm's phones started to melt.

In the year following the drugs scandal, she became the face of an incredible fourteen simultaneous advertising campaigns, netting her £30 million pounds on top of her already enormous modelling earnings. Her contracts included Rimmel cosmetics, Virgin mobile phones, Nikon cameras, Stella McCartney, Belstaff, Versace and Burberry womanswear, Longchamps handbags, Louis Vuitton luggage, Bulgari and David Yurman jewellery, Calvin Klein jeans and Christian Dior accessories. Why? Because she was the girl of the moment. Infamy and fame have a relationship as blurred and hazy as Kate and Pete's own, but that's not important. What mattered was that everyone knew her and a lot of people admired her not for being a junkie but the way she had weathered the storm of the exposé. The coke scandal had the press and public sitting up and looking in her direction like never before.

In addition to the raft of advertising opportunities, billionaire Philip Green began courting her and signed her up for a £3 million contract to design a range of clothes for Topshop, fashion hipsters' favourite High Street store. Her decision to move into design reflects the reality that as a model she running out of time but the image of HER design could sell product every bit as well as wearing it on the catwalk. The corpulent Green put it in a nutshell:

'Kate has a unique position as a true fashion icon.'

Moss' Topshop deal was a collection launched by the Croydon-connection. Green and Moss both hail from there and provided the driving motive to make enough money to get out and never go back. It's a place that figures on anyone's Crap Map and, when Ricky Gervaise did a gig there, it made him wish he'd sited The Office there and not Slough.

It began in Annabel's - the jodhpur set's Mayfair nightclub of choice - when in mid-May 2006 Green bought a charity-auctioned kiss from Kate Moss for £60,000. He decided that as he was with his wife Tina (all his money is lodged with her in Monaco) he would give the kiss to Jemima Khan whom Kate undoubtedly preferred to kiss than Green. What most thought would be a peck on the cheek for the Foundation for Palestinian refugee children turned into a 60-second les-fest. In fact, one ogling hack said the kiss was the first time he'd witnessed female tonsilatio. Billionaire Green looked on amused but not aroused.

Fast forward a fortnight to the bar of the China Tang restaurant, which boasts no Monosodium glutamate, in the basement of the Dorchester Hotel and as Green was leaving he bumped into nightowl Kate who was arriving. She said to him about the £60,000 he'd paid for her to lick Jemima Khan's tonsils, 'That was a bit of fun.'

Motor-mouthed Green, who is never short of a quip, replied, 'I suppose it all depends on your idea of fun.'

She then said, 'I'm a girl from Croydon, you're a boy from Croydon, why don't we do something together?' The wary Green thought to himself that whatever she was going to suggest it would not be going back to Croydon. He asked, 'What do you have you in mind?' She replied:

'I've always wanted to do my own clothing collection.'

A relieved Green trotted out one of his catchphrases, 'Come up and see me.' He fished out his business card with his private number on it and handed it to her, thinking that would be the last he would hear of it. However, Kate was serious and she rang a few days later and, in June 2006, they met in his West End office where she pitched the idea of her collection.

Green knew he could turn her idea into another money spinner but he also knew Kate could be flaky and, as her Cocaine Kate scandal and her courtship of Pete Doherty had proved, a liability. He took his time on this one… three months.

He said, 'I was not interested in doing the kind of one-hit wonder that H&M had [in 2005] with Stella McCartney, selling a few thousand items to a one-off scrum of shoppers. My starting point was this: does Kate have the desire, drive and potential to build a long-term brand? And despite her charm, and the impressive way she came across at our first face-to-face meeting, I was unconvinced.'

Mr Buyout as Green is dubbed in the City for his eye for turning round seemingly burnt-out clothing companies is reckoned to be one of the sharpest businessmen in the country. His Arcadia Group is home to such high street chains such as BHS, Topshop, Topman, Burton, Wallis, Miss Selfridge and Dorothy Perkins. He makes a lot of money and spends it, too, on expensive boats, jets and lavish Caribbean parties. He was knighted in June 2006 for funding a number of educational projects to the tune of £6 million. If anyone asks him if knighthoods can be bought, he responds with another one of his catchphrases, 'Once upon a time...'

What he needed to be convinced of to ride a mass-market Kate Moss clotheshorse was that she would toe the line for what his brainstorming of the idea had convinced him could make his Arcadia Group the UK's leading womanswear retailer. To emphasise the importance of her keeping her edgy, dark side under control he repeatedly told her that this deal could lead to an even more lucrative career than her modelling.

He had her and Storm head Sarah Doukas in to impress on

them both how much it was in their interests for Kate to
shape up and commit. He wanted a multi-million pound Kate
Moss mass-market collection, not haute couture but demi-
couture or, what fashion journalists call, 'cheap-chic'.
The brand could go global because Kate's reach was just
that, whereas Green's chain was still largely UK based. He
stressed that her £3 million deal on the table could be
chicken-feed if everyone kept on message. The UK women's
fashion market turns over approximately £10 billion a year.
The potential of the Kate Moss brand was too good not to
convince Green himself to take the risk on her. His sessions
with her and Doukas convinced him that the deal met his own
business mantra:

I don't do risk –
I do educated risk.

On 20 September 2006, Green and Moss announced the launch
of the Kate Moss Topshop collection. The deal was worth
more than £3 million to Kate as she was also guaranteed
royalties on sales. That night they all returned to China
Tang, where it all started, and Green recalled, 'The Cristal
was flowing. Its not everyday you sign up Kate Moss! She is
a fashion icon in terms of the UK... and this is what Topshop
is all about in terms of fashion. Our customers identify
with her. I felt like I'd done something unique. When we
came out, it seemed like the world's press was there; 45
flashbulbs going off at once.'

Kate with Philip Green at the London Fashion Week show, September 2007

Although Kate's romantic nostalgia for Pete Doherty still kept his corpse twitching for roughly a year, from this point on he was effectively dead as a possible Mr Right.

The Arcadia design-team went into a frenzy as Green detailed in an April 2007 launch for the Kate Moss collection. And he meant in the stores not on the catwalk. Once design was agreed on, there was sourcing fabrics and making production templates before the sweatshops in the far East began work. How much input Kate actually had is a moot point with design experts saying hardly any and the Arcadia Group and her claiming she was closely involved. Obviously being a catwalk queen is no substitute for a three-year slog at design school. She has no grasp of the interrelationships between costs of materials, production and marketing but nearly twenty years in the business has given her more than a schooling in the fundamentals. Moreover, as some fashion critics pointed out, the collection was not so much designed but modelled on Kate Moss' own wardrobe.

The New York Post headlined an article DUPLIKATE with the comment, 'The line she's delivered looks like Kate copying a lot of other people's stuff Kate's worn before.' This was to spectacularly miss the point. Green's whole play was to produce and retail Moss lookalike gear, which he reckoned would fly off the shelves. One of the few fashion commentators to get the point was Richard Hyman of the retail research consultancy Verdict. He pointed out that the strength of the collection was precisely its lack of originality.

He pointed out:

> 'The fashion journalist's grasp of what works in the mass market is not that great. You don't want leading-edge catwalk fashions in a high street store.'

A month before the launch Vogue featured Kate modelling six outfits from her collections with comments, too, on how she put it together: 'I kind of got bits from my closet. We started dragging things out I liked. We looked at stuff and I said, "Well, what if it was like this or that, and in this fabric or that?"' In fact, Green got one of his top stylists, Katie England, to translate Kate's ideas and wardrobe into the 80-piece collection, ranging in price from £12 t0 £200 that went on sale on 1 May 2007 in 227 Topshop outlets.

Green had Kate on parade both for his preview the evening before at his flagship Oxford Street outlet and in the morning at 7.30 a.m. where she more than showed the wear and tear of the night's partying. She even posed in the shop's window.

The frockaholics ran amok: many of the shops sold out on the first day. It did as well in New York where the collection was sold in Barneys and eleven of its subsidiaries. Green had said before the launch, 'This is a major initiative for us, and we want to push the boat along in a big way.' He did exactly that and made a killing.

Meanwhile Kate was still seeing Pete Doherty in an on-off way and, just before the launch, there was even some wedding dress talk. In March they also recorded a cringey homemade video track that Pete posted on YouTube. It is more accurate to call it installation art than rock. He plays guitar while she mouths such obscenities as: 'Rot in jail you cunt. Rot, rot, rot, rot, rot, rot, fuckface'. Showing her rock'n'roll age, Kate concedes on the video, 'Sonny and Cher we're not.'

However, Pete was still on drugs and selling stories about her to buy them. He was also proving to be incapable of taking them without being busted by the Met and it was clearly going to end in an increasingly exasperated judiciary sending him to prison. The shambolic soap opera of his life inevitably rubbed off on her own image, much to the fury of her mother, Doukas and Green. She had cooled the romance around the time of the launch but in August made at attempt at a reconciliation, which turned into a druggies tea-party at Claridge's hotel in Mayfair... with Kate footing a humongous bill. The suite she hired was £2,000 a night!

Inevitably Pete's drug cycle forced the relationship into an off phase and in September they were estranged again. Kate, however, footloose in an obscure rock gig in Camden came across a Doherty lookalike - Jamie Hince, who played guitar in a strange London-based duo called The Kills.

One wag said that when Kate met Hince it was 'lust at first bounce' but, despite all the blasé shrugs at how long it could last, it did. Suddenly, to the relief of everyone around Kate, Pete was history. Unable to top up his drug coffers by selling the tabloids stories about her, Pete was reduced to selling features in which he pleaded for her to come back to him. He said in one their relationship had been like the Vietnam war.

The last six weeks of our relationship were bad. I was always dodging bullets.'

But he concedes it is over and has sought consolation in the arms of the mother of his son Astile, singer-songwriter and genuine 'arch groupie' Lisa Moorish.

Lisa Moorish

7. Hitched to Hince?

With the opening of a new career and the relief of burying Cocaine Kate in the clippings file, Kate began to put herself about publicly. In 2008, she appeared on-stage alongside Matt Lucas for a Comic Relief edition of Little Britain, playing superchav Vicky Pollard's twin sister. Dressed in tracksuit and leggings, draped in fake jewellery, it was a far cry from the catwalk. 'I'm the easy one,' Kate told the audience.

'Total slag. I'm anybody's for a packet of Quavers.'

[Quavers are cheesy-curly crisps made by Walkers.]

When Barneys announced it was taking the Topshop collection it's creative director picked up on her Little Britain motif. He described Kate:

> ## 'She is not a high-born girl. She's a working-class slag from a crap town, like me.'

With the encouragement of Green, she also began to do selected interviews, something she has avoided all her life. Storm ensured that they had copy-approval and no drug questions, but this also was part of the new Kate-brand. Apart from the Vogue interview, which was geared to promoting the Topshop launch, in August she also spoke to Glamour magazine about her child: 'Lila can't be a model until she's at least twenty-one. She is already a mini-me - it is scary. She comes in at bedtime and says, "Mummy, do you think this is a good look?" And then she has a fashion crisis. I say, "You will wear what I tell you" but she says she is the adult of the bedroom. Now we lay the clothes out before she goes to bed but then she goes, "Mum, I need options." She's a mini-me.'

She also said that she wished she had been a musician not a model, 'I would have wanted to be a rock star, a lead singer, if I wasn't a model. I'd go touring in a bus with my band. In my next life, that's the plan.' In this life she seems determined to hook up to one.

JAMIE HINCE

Jamie Hince is no rock star but he is no satellite either. He has his niche in garage rock, although in 2004 he demurred from that label: 'When people compared us with all that, we always felt… not insulted, but we never felt like a garage band. We were more into updating The Velvet Underground's idea of a rock band encompassing all areas of Art and Life.' Jamie is cool, level-headed with a cult following and, most of all, not Pete Doherty or even Doherty-ish.

185

He is a chain-smoking vegan from Andover, now 40, who has been knocking around the punk rock scene for 20 years. He learnt his trade with Brit-bands Blyth Power, then Scarfo, but in 2000 he hooked up with American Allison Mosshart, then 22, who was on tour in the UK with Discount. After some transatlantic touching-up, she came over to his Gypsy Hill pad and they started to live and play together in a duo called The Kills. They work with a drum machine and create a big bluesy-arty sound that isn't that far away from the now disbanded White Stripes. Their stagework, however, is very theatrical, even sexy, and they write all their own songs with him playing guitar more and her dominant on vocals. Both are very reclusive but it seems they broke up as a couple in 2005, after which Jamie took up with French model Valentine Fillol-Cordier. This romance broke down some months before Jamie met Kate.

Certainly, 2008 was a good year for his romance with Kate, although not without its hiccups. Allison Mosshart is not keen on Kate's rock chick persona and initially viewed

her as a little better than a celebrity groupie. She also took offence to Kate's entourage - the Moss Posse - turning up at some of The Kills gigs and stealing the limelight... well 'polluting the atmosphere'. She also didn't like the way when they did turn up someone

was always racking up charlie backstage. Her biggest objection, however, was when Jamie suggested that they use Kate onstage as a kind of crowd-catching gimmick, which she suspected was a stalking horse for giving her a spot in their act. She laid the law down on that: no Kate appearances onstage.

On the other hand Kate knows that Allison and Jamie were an item once and, given the amount of time he necessarily spent with her rehearsing, has had regular jealousy tantrums – what Doherty used to call 'when the wicked witch has one of her napalm days'. In November they came to blows when she attacked him in her St John's Wood home, which they now share, over what she later said was an argument about how they would spend Christmas. Kate explained,

'We had a bit of a scuffle and I was wearing a chunky ring… We fight and we have our ups and downs – like anyone, really.'

January 2009, on holiday in Thailand Kate strokes her baby bump.

Yet, the ups and downs are not all metaphorical because by January they were on holiday in Thailand, with Kate sporting a 'mummy tummy'. It has not been confirmed but there is also talk of marriage.

In 2008, Kate was estimated to be worth some £45 million with annual earnings of £4.5 million.

GREEN

In March 2008 she launched another Topshop fashion collection and before the financial crisis began to bite Green was negotiating with the Chinese to market her line in Beijing, Hong Kong and Shanghai's Superbrand Mall. His Bhs and Arcadia conglomerate actually grew in 2008, bucking the market trend due, in no small measure, to what was called the 'Kate Moss Effect'. In December, Green signed her up for another three years for an undisclosed amount but market analysts say it would be more that her original £3 million a year deal. Her line has now been expanded to include lingerie and some accessories.

Kate said, 'I am really looking forward to working with the Topshop team on our new collections and thank everybody who already owns a piece of Kate Moss for Topshop!'

Green added, 'I believe this has been a great partnership for both Topshop and Kate. Having had two years experience, I am confident that Kate's collection now has the potential to become a significant global brand within Topshop.'

Kate with Jamie outside her St John's Wood home

Meanwhile Green, like a shark sniffing blood, was swimming around the drowned corpses of the womanswear industry. SelectRetail, Ethel Austin, Dolcis and Stead & Simpson folded early in the year, accounting for almost 1,000 stores. Later on in the year, as the Iceland's banking system failed, he was attempting to buy up the debts of chains like Karen Millen and the retail group Baugur at heavily discounted prices. With the retail clothing industry expected to contract by 3% in 2008 many of the companies that had expanded on easy finance in the bumper years will be unable to meet repayments. Debt predators like Green will then be able to buy companies from administration at knockdown prices. Analysts expect him to end 2009 as the biggest womanswear retailer in the country with a not insignificant global reach.

CONCLUSION

Kate Moss hitched herself to Green, who is THE UK player in the clothing market, just as her own catwalk reign in the same industry was coming to an end. Her returns from her deal with Green will eclipse the aggregate earnings of her recent celebrity competitors in highstreet cheap chic: Stella McCartney, Madonna, Lily Allen, Kylie Minogue, et al. It was an extraordinary turn in her fortunes, coming as it did while she was still tarnished with the skank of Doherty and Cocaine Kate.

Luck? Or was it just good timing: being in the right place at the right time with the minimum of effort? If it was luck, she has had an uncanny 21-year run of it from the moment she was headhunted as a 14-year-old by Sarah Doukas and her brother in JFK Airport to, at 35, her present success and wealth. Of course, her widely set eyes, high cheek bones and waif-like body were just a fluke of the genes that Doukas fancied might hit some unfathomable marketing spot. She didn't know the fourteen-year-old had just lost her virginity during the family holiday in the Bahamas but that may have helped contribute to the innocent-but-naughty look that also caught her eye.

Whatever luck discovered her, it wasn't luck that kept her on the magazine covers and catwalks year after year after year until she became an icon of style. Nor was it luck that she popularised skinny jeans, ballet-pumps, mixed gladiator sandals and maxi-dresses, waistcoats and shorts. She upgraded the fashion rules, which became irresistible for the highstreet wannabes when it was combined with her louche-girl cool. Her fellatio-look for the camera, her partying, her rock-chick image... Johnny Depp, even Doherty. Yet her act had its flaws: the slightly bandy legs, the crooked teeth, the messy hair, the chain-smoking, the drunken, stoned paparazzi shots... All ironed out with fuck-off cool. No wonder she shifted product: Kate Moss perfected imperfection.

Donna Karen used her for her 2008 Spring collection campaign and said: 'Kate's wild and sexy and somebody who has the energy to hang out in the streets, to dance... a woman who would have lived in that rawness but with a polish at the same time. The clothes don't wear her, she wears the clothes.' It is no accident that the icon is now a brand.

'People think your success is just a matter of having a pretty face. But it's easy to be chewed up and spat out. You've got to stay ahead of the game to be able to stay in it.'
[Kate Moss, 2007]

CPSIA information can be obtained at www.ICGtesting.com
Printed in the USA
BVOW082217300712

296626BV00013B/47/P